The New York Public Library

Astor, Lenox and Tilden Foundations

Illegal Aliens

THE IMMIGRANT EXPERIENCE

Illegal Aliens

Pierre Hauser

Sandra Stotsky, General Editor
Harvard University Graduate School of Education

CHELSEA HOUSE PUBLISHERS
Philadelphia

CHELSEA HOUSE PUBLISHERS

Editorial Director: Richard Rennert
Production Manager: Pamela Loos
Art Director: Sara Davis
Picture Editor: Judy Hasday

Staff for ILLEGAL ALIENS

Editors: Petra Press and Reed Ueda
Associate Editor: Therese De Angelis
Editorial Assistant: Kristine Brennan
Designer: Alison Burnside
Cover Illustration: Jane Sterrett

First Printing
1 3 5 7 9 8 6 4 2

Library of Congress Cataloging-in-Publication Data

Hauser, Pierre (Pierre N.)
    Illegal Aliens/ Pierre N. Hauser.
    p. cm. – (The Immigrant Experience)
    Includes bibliographical references and index.
    Summary: Examines the history of undocumented immigration to the
United States, the hardships endured by illegal aliens, their motives in immi-
grating, and current efforts to control this situation.
    ISBN 0-7910-3363-5 (hc.)
        0-7910-3385-6 (pbk.)
    1. Illegal aliens–United States–History–Juvenile Literature. 2. Illegal aliens–
Government policy–United States–Juvenile literature. 3. United States–
Emigration and immigration–Government policy–Juvenile literature. [1. Illegal
aliens. 2. United States–Emigration and immigration.] I. Title. II. Series.
JV6493.H38 1996   95-23636
325.73–dc20   CIP
                                                AC

CONTENTS

THE IMMIGRANT EXPERIENCE

CHELSEA HOUSE PUBLISHERS

A
NATION OF
NATIONS

DANIEL PATRICK MOYNIHAN

The Constitution of the United States begins: "We the People of the United States. . ." Yet, as we know, the United States was not then and is not now made up of a single group of people. It is made up of many peoples. Immigrants and bondsmen from Europe, Asia, Africa, and Central and South America came here or were brought here, and still they come. They forged one nation and made it their own. More than 100 years ago, Walt Whitman expressed this great central fact of America: "Here is not merely a nation, but a teeming Nation of nations."

Although the ingenuity and acts of courage of these immigrants, our ancestors, shaped the North American way of life, we sometimes take their contributions for granted. This fine series, *The Peoples of North America*, examines the experiences and contributions of different immigrant groups and how these contributions determined the future of the United States and Canada.

Immigrants did not abandon their ethnic traditions when they reached the shores of North America. Each ethnic group had its own customs and traditions, and each brought different experiences, accomplishments, skills, values, styles of dress, and tastes in food that lingered long after its arrival. Yet this profusion of differences created a singularity, or bond, among the immigrants.

The United States and Canada are unusual in this respect. Whereas religious and ethnic differences have sparked intolerance throughout the rest of the world—from the 17th-century religious wars to the 19th-century nationalist movements in Europe to the near extermination of the Jewish people under Nazi Germany—North Americans have struggled to learn how to respect each other's differences and live in harmony.

Our two countries are hardly the only two in which different groups must learn to live together. There is no nation of significant size anywhere in the world which would not be classified as multiethnic. But only in North America are there so *many* different groups, most of them living cheek by jowl with one another.

This is not easy. Look around the world. And it has not always been easy for us. Witness the exclusion of Chinese immigrants, and for practical purposes Japanese also, in the late 19th century. But by the late 20th century, Chinese and Japanese Americans were the most successful of all the groups recorded by the census. We have had prejudice aplenty, but it has been resisted and recurrently overcome.

The remarkable ability of Americans to live together as one people was seriously threatened by the issue of slavery. Thousands of settlers from the British Isles had arrived in the colonies as indentured servants, agreeing to work for a specified number of years on farms or as apprentices in return for passage to America and room and board. When the first Africans arrived in the then-British colonies during the 17th century, some colonists thought that they too should be treated as indentured servants. Eventually, the question of whether the Africans should be treated as indentured, like the English, or as slaves who could be owned for life was considered in a Maryland court. The court's calamitous decree held that blacks were slaves bound to a lifelong servitude, and so also were their children. America went through a time of moral examination and civil war before it finally freed African slaves and their descendants. The principle that all people are created equal had faced its greatest challenge and survived.

Yet the court ruling that set blacks apart from other races fanned flames of discrimination that burned long after slavery was abolished—and that still flicker today. Indeed, it was about the time of the American Civil War that European theories of evolution were turned to the service of ranking different peoples by their presumed distance from our apelike ancestors.

When the Irish flooded American cities to escape the famine in Ireland, the cartoonists caricatured the typical "Paddy" (a common term for Irish immigrants) as an apelike creature with jutting jaw and sloping forehead.

By the 20th century, racism and ethnic prejudice had given rise to virulent theories of a Northern European master race. When Adolf Hitler came to power in Germany in 1933, he popularized the notion of an Aryan race. Only a man of the deepest ignorance and evil could have done this. *Aryan* is a Sanskrit word, which is to say the ancient script of what we now think of as India. It means "noble" and was adopted by linguists—notably by a fine German scholar, Max Müller—to denote the Indo-European family of languages. Müller was horrified that anyone could think of it in terms of race, especially a race of blond-haired, blue-eyed Teutons. But the Nazis embraced the notion of a master race. Anyone with darker and heavier features was considered inferior. Buttressed by these theories, the German Nazi state from 1933 to 1945 set out to destroy European Jews, along with Poles, Gypsies, Russians, and other groups considered inferior. It nearly succeeded. Millions of these people were murdered.

The tragedies brought on by ethnic and racial intolerance throughout the world demonstrate the importance of North America's efforts to create a society free of prejudice and inequality.

A relatively recent example of the New World's desire to resolve ethnic friction nonviolently is the solution that the Canadians found to a conflict between two ethnic groups. A long-standing dispute as to whether Canadian culture was properly English or French resurfaced in the mid-1960s, dividing the peoples of the French-speaking Province of Quebec from those of the English-speaking provinces. Relations grew tense, then bitter, then violent. The Royal Commission on Bilingualism and Biculturalism was established to study the growing crisis and to propose measures to ease the tensions. As a result of the commission's recommendations, all official documents and statements from the national government's capital at Ottawa are now issued in both French and English, and bilingual education is encouraged.

The year 1980 marked a coming of age for the United States's ethnic heritage. For the first time, the U.S. Bureau of the Census asked people about their ethnic background. Americans chose from more than 100 groups, including French Basque, Spanish Basque, French Canadian, African-American, Peruvian, Armenian, Chinese, and Japanese. The ethnic group with the largest response was English (49.6 million). More than 100 million Americans claimed ancestors from the British Isles, which includes England, Ireland, Wales, and Scotland. There were almost as many Germans (49.2 million) as English. The Irish-American population (40.2 million) was third, but the next-largest ethnic group, the African-Americans, was a distant fourth (21 million). There was a sizable group of French ancestry (13 million) as well as of Italian (12 million). Poles, Dutch, Swedes, Norwegians, and Russians followed. These groups, and other smaller ones, represent the wondrous profusion of ethnic influences in North America.

Canada too has learned more about the diversity of its population. Studies conducted during the French/English conflict showed that Canadians were descended from Ukrainians, Germans, Italians, Chinese, Japanese, native Indians, and Inuit, among others. Canada found it had no ethnic majority, although nearly half of its immigrant population had come from the British Isles. Canada, like the United States, is a land of immigrants for whom mutual tolerance is a matter of reason as well as principle. But note how difficult this can be in practice, even for persons of manifest goodwill.

The people of North America are the descendants of one of the greatest migrations in history. And that migration is not over.

Koreans, Vietnamese, Nicaraguans, Cubans, and many others are heading for the shores of North America in large numbers. This mix of cultures shapes every aspect of our lives. To understand ourselves, we must know something about our diverse ethnic ancestry. Nothing so defines the North American nations as the motto on the Great Seal of the United States: *E Pluribus Unum*—Out of Many, One.

Two young Mexicans, presumably illegal aliens, cross the U.S. border near Tijuana, Mexico. It is estimated that in the 1980s as many as 10 million immigrants entered the United States illegally.

A GROWING PROBLEM

U nited States government figures show that each year in the 1990s more than 900,000 new immigrants have become legal, permanent residents of the United States. In addition, an estimated 300,000 persons have become illegal residents, either by slipping across a border without identification or by overstaying a legally obtained student, worker, or tourist visa. By 1996, the total estimated number of illegals residing in the United States was four million, most of whom entered the country after 1986.

Despite the increasing efforts of the federal government to crack down on illegals, relatively few have been apprehended. In 1995, a record 51,600 were caught and deported, a 15 percent increase from the previous year. Yet the number of people caught is hardly a trickle compared to the tens of thousands streaming into the country each year. The 1990s have also shown a new pattern of illegal migration, as more and more illegal aliens have settled in cities and small towns in the Midwest.

Many Americans are seriously questioning the appropriateness and effectiveness of America's current immigration policy. In fact, this issue is presenting the nation with one of its most serious and controversial challenges.

On one end of the spectrum are those who oppose all immigration, legal and illegal. They argue that America is no longer the wide-open frontier it was 150 years ago, when it had the space and job opportunities to welcome new settlers. They want a harsh crackdown on illegal immigrants already living in the United States and stronger measures to keep future illegals out. But they also want the annual flow of legal immigrants stopped or strongly curtailed. Their reasons: to protect the U.S. work force and to prevent an increase in the tax burden they believe immigrants stimulate as a result of increased welfare and health services. Some people with extreme views want to prevent the large numbers of Hispanic and Asian immigrants from "diluting" the national character because they supposedly do not assimilate as easily as earlier European generations did.

At the other extreme are those who want immigration restrictions lifted and the doors opened even further to newcomers. They point to the cultural and social contributions immigrants have traditionally made to the United States and cite statistics to prove that immigrants consistently stimulate the American economy with tax dollars far more than they drain it with a demand for public education, welfare, and health services. While they admit that the number of illegals arriving each year has become overwhelming and costly, they believe that America has a moral obligation to provide political shelter and economic opportunity for the world's persecuted and destitute masses, whether they come with permission or not. To them, an illegal alien is a poor, often desperate person in need of food, shelter, a job, and whatever else it takes to start a new life in a safe place. Extreme immigration advocates also believe that all immigrants—legal and illegal—should be accorded the same rights and opportunities and have access to the same benefits and public aid as U.S. citizens have, especially for their children. Many people with this viewpoint go so far as to paint people who want to deport illegal aliens as racist.

About the only thing most people agree on is that immigration laws need to be changed and that illegal immigration needs to be eliminated. Obviously, a fair and balanced policy lies somewhere between the two extremes.

Who Are Our Illegal Aliens?

Illegal aliens did not become a significant problem until World War II, when the United States started importing temporary Mexican laborers to ease its labor shortage. By the late 1960s and early 1970s, Mexicans represented more than 90 percent of all illegal aliens living in the United States. But in the 1980s the illegal alien population of America began to change dramatically, as large groups started to arrive from more than 40 nations throughout the world. Most have come from impoverished or politically troubled nations in the Western Hemisphere, particularly Nicaragua, Guatemala, El Salvador, Haiti, Colombia, and the Dominican Republic. But sizable contingents have also been arriving illegally from European countries such as Ireland and Poland and Asian countries such as China, together with a much smaller number from Middle Eastern nations such as Israel and Iran.

Large-scale immigration is not new. The United States is a nation built by immigrants, many of whom arrived in an "open door" era, when there were no quotas and few restrictions. In fact, everyone in this country is either an immigrant from another country or continent, or the descendant of immigrants. This includes members of the 500 or so Native American cultures that were thriving in North America when the first Europeans arrived; anthropologists believe they were the descendants of people who migrated from Asia over a land bridge at the Bering Strait during the

Ice Age and then settled in North, Central, and South America. (Africans brought to the Americas as slaves are not considered immigrants because they did not come to this country by choice.)

In most cases, these immigrants came either because they were urged to immigrate by family members who had arrived earlier or because farmers, mining concerns, railroad companies, and other businesses urgently needed labor. Wherever they came from, all were considered "different" when they first arrived. In addition, they were often viewed with suspicion by those citizens who feared the impact the newcomers might have on the nation's economy and culture. Many Americans felt that immigrants who were at best barely literate and who had little experience with the workings of democratic self-government (such as those from eastern or southern European countries, for example, or from China) could never fit in because they would not be able to adapt to a representative form of self-government. In contrast, immigration from other ethnic and religious groups, especially Protestant groups from northern and western Europe, was viewed with less concern.

Like every other nation, the United States has had to formulate an immigration policy that involves more than an open door to newcomers from foreign countries. It is both the right and the responsibility of a democratic nation to manage immigration so that it best serves the national interest. Thus, American legislators have been required to draft laws and guidelines that help reunite families, enrich the country's cultural heritage, stand up for the nation's tradition of religious and humanitarian values, and provide a haven for the persecuted—while helping and protecting the nation's economy.

Fear and prejudice have certainly played a part in the drafting of immigration legislation during America's 200-year history. Yet most immigration laws have been drafted in what legislators hoped were the best economic interests of the country. Then, as now, legislators have had to grapple with important questions, such as: How can we ensure that immigration is based on and supports our broad national economic, social, and humanitarian interests rather than the interests of a powerful few who seek gain by violating or exploiting our laws? How can we gain effective control over our borders—which every nation must have in order to maintain its security—and still encourage international trade, investment, and tourism? How can we maintain common values and a civic culture based on the concepts of individual rights and individual responsibilities, while still accommodating a large and diverse immigrant population? To how many of the world's refugees can we be a safe haven?

In other words, how can we make sure that the people who should get in do get in, the people who should not get in are kept out, and the people who should be deported are required to leave? These issues are more crucial now than they have been at any other time in U.S. history.

From 1980 to 1990, three major pieces of legislation were adopted in an attempt to overhaul America's immigration policy: the Refugee Act of 1980, the Immigration Reform and Control Act of 1986, and the Immigration Act of 1990. These laws were aimed at rectifying the flaws and inequities of previous immigration legislation. They were intended to serve the national interest by helping reunite immigrant families, by providing U.S. employers access to job skills not available in the U.S. labor force, and by defining a humanitarian refugee system that supports international refugee law. They were also designed to implement a stronger enforcement system (through employer sanctions and tighter border control) to deter illegal immigration. While these laws have alleviated some of the immigration problems facing the country today, they have been less than effective on others. Most Americans agree that more reforms are needed.

A U.S. border patrolman and a paramedic aid a young Salvadoran woman who was overcome by heat exhaustion and thirst in the Arizona desert in July 1980 after entering the United States illegally. Because the situation in their homeland is often so desperate, immigrants are willing to take great risks to enter the United States.

The Politics of Immigration

Few U.S. citizens would argue about the need for secure borders. Most Americans want legal immigration into the country to continue but feel that reforms are needed regarding quotas, procedures, and the nation's policy toward political refugees. Most people also want illegal immigration stopped. More controversial are the kinds and degrees of reforms being proposed for legal immigration and the methods being proposed to end illegal immigration.

It would be a mistake simply to categorize liberals as pro-immigration and conservatives as promoters of increased immigration restrictions, or to split the issue between Democrats and Republicans. Labor unions believe, for example, that immigration, both legal and illegal, depresses wages and takes away jobs from unskilled Americans and should therefore be stopped, or at least strongly restricted. Illegals currently residing in the United States, labor unions say, should be tracked down and deported.

Many business owners, on the other hand, are strongly pro-immigration. President Bill Clinton and others who supported the passage of the North American Free Trade Agreement (NAFTA) believed that the free flow of people over national borders, like that of goods and capital, could only lead to prosperity. House majority leader Dick Armey was another major proponent of this ideology, as has been the editorial board of the *Wall Street Journal*. (Some of these free-market supporters argue against a crackdown on legal immigrants, saying that the best way to combat illegal immigration in the United States is to open the country's gates wider to legal entrants.)

Patrick J. Buchanan, a conservative Republican who sought the presidency in 1996, and other opponents of free-market legislation have said that the United States was wrong to sign the NAFTA, claiming that not only has it failed to slow illegal immigration, it has resulted in lost American jobs.

Other employers, including many ranchers in Texas and California, are fed up with illegal immigration from Mexico and are adamantly anti-immigration. Despite Operation Gatekeeper, a border-fortification mission enacted in the early 1990s, the illegals keep coming. A few episodes of vigilantism by ranchers have erupted, leading authorities to issue a public request that residents not take the law into their own hands.

Anti-immigration sentiment also comes from "nativists," Americans who want all non-European immigration stopped and all illegals currently residing in the United States deported. They believe that descendants of the English and Scots-Irish Protestants who settled in the 13 colonies are the country's true "natives" and that the large influx of immigrants—both legal and illegal—from Latin America are a threat to America's political heritage and culture.

Hispanic-American groups are also often strong advocates of tighter immigration restrictions. According to the 1990 Latino National Political Survey, a survey of three national Hispanic groups residing throughout the United States (people of Mexican, Puerto Rican, and Cuban origins), an overwhelming majority of the Hispanic population in America believes that there is too much legal as well as illegal immigration. Rodolfo O. de la Garza, professor of government at the University of Texas in Austin and the survey's principal researcher, explained that "Latinos are the people who feel the greatest economic competition from immigrants."

On the other hand, the Asian American Association, established by Marty Shih in the mid-1990s, is pro-immigration, believing that if the restrictive bills pending in Congress became law "there would be a negative impact on the Asian community." Strongly pro-family, members of the Asian community want relatives to join them from overseas, and they want their culture replenished with new arrivals. The association mails out pro-immigration materials nationwide in five Asian languages, urging readers to contact their congressional representatives.

Many Christian fundamentalists are also strongly pro-family and are taking a liberal pro-immigration stance for that reason. They assert that the proposal to end or restrict immigration for the parents and siblings of American citizens (or other legal U.S. residents) is "anti-family" and therefore against traditional American values.

There are those who support anti-immigration measures who feel the government has not taken enough control to make effective changes. Dan Stein, executive director of the Federation for American Immigration Reform (FAIR), charged that legislation pending in Congress in 1996 only "fueled taxpayer costs and public frustration" because 1) the system it proposed to verify legal alien status for employers was not strong enough, and 2) the bill was "turning its back on the American worker" by not restricting legal immigration levels to 300,000 a year or less (preferably much less) and by refusing to set definite caps on the number of political refugees the United States can take in each year.

A number of people living in California, Texas, Florida, and New York—states that bear the overwhelming brunt of illegal immigration costs—believe that all immigration should be stopped or sharply restricted and that the federal government should crack down on illegal immigration and deport those who are already in the country. They also hold that federal tax dollars should underwrite overburdened state social, health, and welfare organizations. Many people in other states believe that the problem is strictly a state issue and are outraged at the suggestion that their federal tax dollars should be used this way. Senator Dianne Feinstein, a California Democrat, has lobbied strongly for the federal government to share California's illegal alien tax burden. (Some people believe that states are not given equal consideration by the federal government. California governor Pete Wilson, for example, criticized President Clinton in August 1994 for moving quickly to stop Cubans from illegally entering Florida while ignoring the much larger and costlier problem of illegal immigration in California.)

Meanwhile, groups like the National Rifle Association (NRA) are strongly pro-immigration because they are skeptical of any programs that might give the federal government too much control. They adamantly oppose some of the programs Congress is proposing to control illegal immigration, such as

In this photograph from 1963, a border patrolman trains his binoculars on the Rio Grande, the river on the Texas-Mexico border that many immigrants use to enter the United States. In the 1990s, the Border Patrol is as likely to use sophisticated computers, radar, and sensors as binoculars.

mandatory national identification cards or a computerized national registry of Social Security numbers that employers would have to check before hiring someone. "The N.R.A. position is simple," said Grover Norquist, executive director of Americans for Tax Reform, in December 1995. "If you're going to register people, why not guns?"

Some politicians changed their positions on immigration radically in the 1990s. During his eight years as a U.S. senator, Pete Wilson wrote hundreds of letters to immigration officials on behalf of foreign workers whom authorities wanted to deport. Yet governor Pete Wilson's short-lived presidential campaign in 1995 was built on his opposition to illegal immigration.

To the American Civil Liberties Union (ACLU) and other prominent civil rights advocacy organizations, immigration is often a human-rights issue. Such groups generally oppose most immigration limits and restrictions and believe that legal and illegal immigrants alike should enjoy most of the rights and have access to all the public services enjoyed by American citizens.

Many environmentalists and population control advocates, on the other hand, want all immigration stopped or severely restricted. They feel that increases in the American population due to immigration will cause overpopulation, which in turn will prevent Americans from being able to preserve their environment and protect their quality of life. According to the Roper Poll, commissioned by Negative Population Growth, a nonprofit group that advocates a substantially decreased U.S. population, 79 percent of those polled said that even legal immigration should be scaled back to 300,000 or less annually. Fifty-four percent of those endorsed limits of 100,000 or less.

Immigration Commission Appointed

In 1993, in an effort to reconcile all of these viewpoints, President Clinton announced a multiyear strategy to regain control of the nation's borders and to guard America's tradition of legal immigration by enacting more effective measures to deter and prevent illegal immigration. In the President's Report to Congress in 1994, Clinton stated, "The Administration's goal is to stop illegal immigrants, welcome legal immigrants, and protect refugees from harm." To do that, the administration sought to have Congress pass a series of laws that strengthened border control, deported criminal aliens, developed a computerized criminal alien tracking center, reduced work incentives for illegal aliens, stopped asylum abuse by nonpolitical refugees, revitalized the Immigration and Naturalization Service (INS), and encouraged legal aliens to become naturalized citizens.

Perhaps even more important to the subject of immigration has been the creation in 1990 of a commission to study the immigration issue, hear all the differing viewpoints, and then recommend strong and positive reforms before further legislation is to be enacted. The commission is to analyze the failures of the nation's current immigration policy and to make appropriate recommendations not just for the present, but for the future. (Chapter 6 takes a closer look at the commission and its recommendations.)

It does not take a special commission to figure out that one of the reasons the current immigration system is such a bewildering and infuriating maze to many Americans is its confusing alien classification system.

Confusing "Alien" Definitions

By basic definition, an alien is a person living in a country other than the one in which he or she was born. Yet there are so many differences in the legal status of various aliens in the United States that even immigration authorities and the immigrants themselves have trouble understanding the rules. For example, an alien can be a lawful permanent resident without citizenship status, a political refugee, someone who has applied for but not yet received political refugee status, or a person residing in the United States under such laws as the Chinese Student Protection Act or the Cuban Adjustment Act.

The word *alien* is sometimes even used to describe foreign-born Americans with citizenship status. An alien could also be a member of one of a number of temporary resident categories, including workers and students on temporary visas, diplomats, tourists, crew members, representatives of foreign media, and intra-company transferees. People in all of these categories are considered legal aliens—that is, as long as their visas have not expired.

To many Americans, the term *illegal alien* conjures up a stereotypical image of a ragged young Mexican sneaking across the U.S.-Mexican border, probably by swimming across the Rio Grande or by climbing over a barbed-wire fence. According to 1995 estimates of the Immigration and Naturalization Service, a substantial number of undocumented aliens do enter the United States by illegally crossing the border. These are mostly single young men or women who buy forged green cards (identification cards certifying that an alien has permanent resident status) on the black market once they arrive so they can work in the States. But INS figures show that the majority of illegals arrive in the United States by a much different route. It is estimated that at least 60 percent of the country's annual new influx of illegal aliens are people who enter the country legally on temporary work, study, or visitation visas and then stay on permanently after their visas expire. These are aliens who start out legal, then lose their legal status.

To make the classification of aliens even more confusing, the Immigration Reform and Control Act provided amnesty in 1986 to all undocumented aliens who could prove they had lived in the United States continuously since 1982 or earlier. Those who qualified were given temporary resident status for 18 months, after which they were eligible for permanent resident status and then, after another five years, citizenship. The law also had provisions of amnesty for alien farm workers who could prove they worked in the United States at least 90 days during the period from May 1, 1985, to May 1, 1986.

While this legislation was applauded by many Americans because it helped reduce the exploitation of undocumented farm workers, others held that it actually increased illegal immigration. Thousands more illegals tried to cross the U.S.-Mexican border to see if they could qualify for the amnesty with false papers. Former illegals who were granted amnesty now felt safer smuggling in family members they had left behind.

Illegals Present Major Social Concerns

Although illegal aliens, like most American citizens and lawful immigrants, generally abide by the law, their unlawful entry or the overstaying of their visas is a serious violation of a federal law that was designed in the best national interest.

Moreover, the presence of illegals often promotes crime. Illegals frequently become an exploitable underclass who are reluctant to report crimes committed against them for fear of being deported. Organized crime, especially, preys on the desperate desire of people to enter or remain in the United States through exploitative smuggling and counterfeiting rings. In early 1996, for example, INS officials broke up a multi-million-dollar, counterfeit-document ring that operated in at least six states. A two-year investigation and an elaborate "sting" operation resulted in the arrest of nine Mexican nationals, including a man considered by many to be the "godfather" of illegal immigration in Los Angeles.

INS commissioner Doris Meisner reported in early 1996, "This is nasty stuff and a lot of money is being made out of it." She cited a price of $28,000 charged by one gang to bring an immigrant from Moscow to south Texas via Nicaragua and Mexico. "People get killed doing this," Meisner added. "There is extortion, rape, bribery, abuse of a very serious kind."

Many people believe that illegal immigration also encourages social crimes such as robbery, drug dealing, and gang warfare among those who are unemployed and living in overcrowded slums.

Illegals are also often illegally exploited by unscrupulous employers who violate labor standards with low wages and abusive working conditions to undercut their competition. Many U.S. citizens—and a large majority of legal aliens—resent illegals for taking jobs they believe would otherwise be held by citizens or lawful immigrants.

Another serious and controversial social problem

caused by illegal aliens is the expensive assistance they often require in the form of emergency health and welfare benefits. Many pregnant mothers enter the country illegally because their children become legal American citizens if they are born on American soil and then qualify for welfare benefits. At present, the children of illegal aliens living in the United States are also entitled to a public education in schools paid for by legal resident taxpayers, and they often require special programs to teach them English. According to Government Accounting Office figures released in 1996, the total cost of providing state services for illegal immigrants in California was $2.351 billion, including $1.596 billion for education, $.395 billion for medical services, and $.36 billion for prison. The estimated state and local taxes illegals paid amounted to $.878 billion, leaving a net cost to the state of $1.437 billion.

Illegal aliens also undermine America's commitment to legal immigration. Many Americans have become so frustrated with what they see as the social problems and tax liabilities caused by illegal aliens that they are beginning to demand that all immigration—legal and illegal—be stopped or sharply curtailed.

A Worldwide Issue

The United States is not the only country today that is forced to deal with immigration issues. In fact, every industrialized nation is currently struggling with the social, cultural, and financial repercussions of an influx of foreigners, especially illegal immigrants from poor, politically unstable, and often war-torn countries.

Europe has been overwhelmed with asylum seekers and illegal immigrants from northern Africa, sub-Saharan Africa, eastern Europe, and the Middle East. Japan is witnessing a torrent of illegals from China and other southeast Asian countries. In the last few years, large numbers of people have fled their war-torn homelands of Somalia, Rwanda, Iraq, Bosnia, Croatia, Haiti, Afghanistan, Tajikistan, Azerbaijan, and Armenia, to

Nativism is not just a concept from 19th-century American history. This photograph from 1975 shows angry construction workers stopping traffic on the Brooklyn Bridge to protest layoffs in the construction industry. Several are carrying signs expressing their belief that illegal immigrants are taking American jobs, a sentiment that dates almost to the beginning of immigration to the United States.

name just a few. Even struggling nations are burdened with refugees and illegals. Zaire has had to deal with hundreds of thousands of refugees from Rwanda, Pakistan with an influx from Afghanistan, India from Bangladesh, and Thailand from Burma and Cambodia.

The United States is one of the few countries in the world populated primarily by immigrants and the descendants of immigrants. (Canada, Argentina, and Australia are others.) It has had to deal with the complex issues of citizenship status, alien rights, political asylum for refugees, and the tensions of a multiethnic society for over 200 years. Today, however, countries like Germany, England, the Netherlands, France, Japan, and South Africa are struggling with those same volatile issues.

No one has an exact count, but authorities estimate that there are currently about 25 million citizens and residents in Europe alone who are immigrants or the descendants of immigrants—a figure that amounts to about 6 percent of Europe's population. That figure, however, does not include immigrants residing there illegally, a widely disputed number that authorities agree ranges in the millions. As the economies of poor countries in Africa, the Middle East, and elsewhere deteriorate and populations continue to increase, political tensions explode and the number of illegal immigrants to Europe continues to rise.

The face of Europe began taking on new color in the 1950s, when many European colonies in Africa and southeast Asia gained independence and Europe welcomed former subjects fleeing the subsequent political turmoil in their newly independent Third World countries. In the economic boom of the 1960s, countries such as Germany and France, which had been unwilling to accept permanent new immigrants on a regular basis, suddenly found themselves with critical labor shortages. They set up temporary worker programs, importing laborers from eastern Europe as well as northern Africa, Turkey, and other struggling Islamic nations.

What Europeans did not realize at the time was how many of these foreign "guest workers" would set down roots, send for their extended families, and stay on as permanent residents after their visas expired, even when European economies began to slump in the 1970s and 1980s and there were no longer any work shortages. The designers of these temporary work programs never dreamed they would be creating large, permanent, non-European subcultures within their native countries. To many Europeans, these are undesirable subcultures with strange languages and disturbing religious and cultural traditions. Many former guest workers are now unemployed or are working at jobs that, some Europeans feel, rightfully belong to their own citizens.

While many large communities of Arab, Turkish, and African immigrants do coexist peacefully within countries such as France, Germany, the Netherlands, Belgium, and England, there are also many instances of racial clashes. Unable to find work and stuck in sprawling slums, some immigrants resort to crime and drug dealing to survive. In certain areas, young immigrants have formed gangs. Fear and resentment of these newcomers have fanned anti-immigrant sentiment. Extremist groups have arisen that blame immigrants (legal and illegal) for Europe's rising rate of crime, gang violence, drug dealing, Islamic religious extremism, and even political terrorism. "Skinheads" and other neo-Nazi hate groups often assault Arab, African, and Turkish immigrants, provoking racial riots. Right-wing European extremists are also gaining power with the rise of ultra-conservative political parties on both the national and local levels.

As in the United States, immigration in Europe is a complicated matter, and European governments have initiated a number of programs aimed at controlling it. At this point, it is expensive and difficult for governments just to keep track of the legal immigrants who have overstayed their visas, let alone set up programs to prevent more from arriving. Governments are also straining to provide health, education, and welfare services to the families of those already there.

In the 1970s, when European industry no longer needed the massive influx of imported labor, governments closed down many of the legal entry points for immigrants. As in the United States, this merely triggered an upsurge of illegal border crossings and visa overstays. Governments then took a more active stance through employer sanctions (making it illegal for employers to hire certain immigrants) and an elaborate and costly identification system requiring national identity cards (a computerized system that the United States is also now considering). Europeans have also come to understand that their governments have to work together if they hope to stem the problem.

Germany succeeded in reducing the flow of refugees across its borders by declaring that it will not accept refugees that come through a "safe" third country, insisting that refugees make their claim for asylum in the first country in which they arrive. Germany classifies "safe" countries as those where there is a presumption that human rights are sufficiently protected, so that no one from that country is likely to have a justifiable claim for asylum. By identifying all of its bordering neighbors as safe countries, Germany has insulated itself against refugee influxes. Other western European governments have followed similar strategies, with the result that the refugee flows from eastern Europe, the former Soviet Union, and the Third World have started to decrease. Illegal immigrants continue to be a major and growing problem, however.

South Africa also has significant problems with refugees and illegals. Each year civil war, famine, and overpopulation drive thousands of people from all over Africa to seek a better life in relatively prosperous South Africa. Some of these immigrants are well-educated professionals who are welcomed as legal immigrants, but the majority of the job-seekers are illiterate peasants who enter the country illegally. In a country already tense with racial conflict, immigration issues are pitting black immigrants against native black citizens who bitterly resent the newcomers for taking away jobs.

As in western Europe, increased prosperity in Japan and Korea created labor shortages that attracted several hundred thousand illegal aliens from neighboring Asian countries, especially China. The governments of Japan and Korea have found it hard to formulate acceptable immigration policies for many of the same reasons that immigration has confounded American policymakers. Citizens are demanding a harsh crackdown on illegals, whom they blame for their countries' social problems, while at the same time many trade and industrial employers are encouraging illegals to stay because they work for lower pay and fewer benefits.

The Growing Worldwide Refugee Problem

International politics has always played a special role in every nation's immigration policy, and the doors have often been opened to help political refugees despite existing quotas or other restrictions. In the late 1940s and early 1950s, for example, the U.S. government admitted more than 50,000 Europeans left homeless by World War II. In the 1970s, the United States admitted more than one million refugees from the Caribbean and Indochina, and in 1980 the U.S. government even passed a refugee act authorizing the State Department to admit over 50,000 political refugees a year (and even more in the event of an emergency).

Nevertheless, controversy continues in the United States and other nations over how many refugees a country can accommodate—and has a moral responsibility to accommodate—and whether refugees who come without permission should be considered illegal aliens and therefore deported. Refugees pose serious financial problems to their receiving countries. Often the communities who take them in are overwhelmed by the burden of providing refugee families with medical care, financial support, education, and assistance in finding jobs and housing.

Another problem countries face is whom to admit and whom to turn away. In addition to the thousands fleeing political persecution or physical catastrophe, there are hundreds of thousands more in poverty-stricken countries such as Nicaragua and Haiti who are desperate to emigrate for economic opportunity. While the plight of these people evokes near-universal sympathy, it is simply not possible for the United States or any other single nation to take in all of the world's poor. So how many immigrants can a country reasonably be expected to accommodate? Who determines whether a person's reason for immigrating is sufficiently political to warrant refugee status? And what if immigrants come anyway? These are painful humani-

tarian issues governments all over the world have to struggle with every day.

Another refugee issue that each government needs to consider is how its foreign policy affects the diplomatic balance of international power. A country's foreign policy (or the foreign policies of its political allies) can strongly influence which nationals it grants refugee status. For example, an industrialized nation that supports the government of a particular poor nation—or has close allies that do— may find it difficult to accept that country's citizens as political refugees because doing so would constitute criticism of the poor nation's government. If the industrialized nation does offer criticism, it risks jeopardizing diplomatic and trade relations not only with the poor nation but with its own allies, even when the accusation that

A masked family of Salvadoran refugees, illegal immigrants, meets the press in September 1983 at the Quaker meeting-house that offered them sanctuary. As the number of illegal immigrants in the United States rose in the 1980s, religious organizations often offered their help to the newcomers.

the poor nation is persecuting its own citizens is legitimate.

Understandably, government leaders throughout the world are beginning to realize that providing a safe haven for refugees is a global issue. As such, it must be addressed at the international level.

Terrorism

Another problem of growing international concern is the use of forged or stolen passports by foreign terrorists. In 1990, for example, the Nicaraguan government realized that 50,000 of the passports it issued could not be accounted for. Nicaragua's president, Violeta Chamorro, immediately ordered a new type of passport to be issued and the old type to be invalidated, but by then the stolen passports had already been sold on the black market and were being used by terrorists to slip in and out of countries all over the world. The investigation of the World Trade Center bombing in 1995 turned up five Nicaraguan passports in the possession of people who had never set foot in that country. And when Iraqi troops withdrew from Kuwait in February 1991, they left behind a large number of Nicaraguan passports.

An Evolving Process

To better understand the issues regarding immigration policy in the United States and what experts are recommending for the coming century, it is best to examine how the United States arrived at its current policies. Who were America's first immigrants? How did immigrants who arrived after 1880 differ from those who arrived earlier? How has immigration changed since World War II? How have different immigrant groups been treated and why? How have immigrants shaped the United States over the last two centuries? Who were the country's first illegal aliens, and how have they been treated? What have immigrants (both legal and illegal) gained by moving here, and what have they lost? What kinds of immigration laws have been passed in this country and what roles have fear and prejudice played in their passage? How effective have these laws been? These and other questions will be answered as the story unfolds.

A NEW COUNTRY
OPENS ITS DOORS

Throughout history, people have left their homelands for one or more of five general reasons: for better economic conditions in which to work and raise a family; to escape political, racial, or religious persecution; to escape physical disaster, such as earthquakes, floods, or famine; to reunite with other family members who had already migrated; or to avoid prosecution for crimes they had committed.

Migration—the flow of people away from their homelands in search of better economic or political opportunities—is a phenomenon as old as the history of humankind. It often creates difficulties, sometimes for the migrants, sometimes for the people they encounter, often for both. At times it can bring great rewards as well.

Some immigrants who came to America before it gained independence from Great Britain in the 18th century—like the Puritans, the Jews, and the Huguenots—sought to escape religious persecution in their own countries. Others, like the early Dutch and certain English settlers, came primarily for economic reasons.

When the United States of America declared itself independent in the late 1700s, it introduced to the

Quarantined Chinese immigrants at Angel Island, California, the chief entry station for immigrants on the West Coast in the late 19th and early 20th centuries.

37

world a new concept of citizenship. The United States was the first nation in which citizenship was based not on a common history, ethnicity, or religion, but on an intellectual commitment to the country's political principles and institutions. Foreign-born immigrants who entered with the permission of the U.S. government had the opportunity to gain full citizenship by swearing an oath to uphold those principles, a procedure known as naturalization.

It is important to note that this revolutionary principle of citizenship did not include the right of any person to enter the United States illegally—that is, without permission—and then to remain to enjoy the protection, benefits, and opportunities that the country made available to its own citizens. No matter how great his or her need, no one was accorded that right, and this principle stands today.

In the early years of the United States, illegal aliens did not exist. Our leaders placed no restrictions whatsoever on immigration—no yearly quotas, no laws excluding specific ethnic groups, no preference systems. No authorities were assigned to monitor traffic coming across borders or into port cities. The "gates" were open to anyone who could afford the trip. This policy of unlimited immigration is sometimes referred to as the "open-door policy."

The open-door policy was formulated in 1793 when the first American president, George Washington, declared:

> The bosom of America is open to receive not only the opulent and respectable stranger, but the oppressed and persecuted of all nations and religions; whom we shall welcome to a participation of all our rights and privileges, if by decency and propriety of conduct they appear to merit the enjoyment.

Under the U.S. Constitution, Congress, not the president, was supposed to regulate immigration. But

because most legislators agreed with Washington's policy, they let it stand. Thereafter, however, immigration policy would be determined largely by Congress.

The framers of the Constitution specifically gave Congress the responsibility of defending national borders, guaranteeing certain rights, drafting and enforcing laws, and ensuring the fair representation of all segments of the population. Statesmen such as Thomas Jefferson and Benjamin Franklin were farsighted enough to realize that America's open-door policy for European immigrants eventually would draw people of many races, nationalities, and religious persuasions, so they also saw to it that Congress had the responsibility to regulate immigration.

The framers believed that without strong and fair regulation, the social, economic, cultural, and demographic repercussions of immigration could eventually throw the country into conflict and chaos. They were right. Except for a few fragmentary, politically motivated pieces of legislation, almost a hundred years

This political cartoon from the late 18th century shows George Washington and a phalanx of troops trampling their political enemies, chief among them Thomas Jefferson and Citizen Genet, France's minister to the United States. Jefferson was a member of the early Republican party and favored close ties with France, whereas Federalist anti-immigration legislation aimed to limit the French influence.

passed before the rapidly expanding country tried to formulate its first real immigration policy.

The First Challenge

In 1798, the nation's first two political parties, the Federalists and the Republicans, disagreed on what official position the United States should take regarding the war between France and England. The Federalists, disturbed by France's seizure of American merchant ships headed for England, called for the United States to renounce the alliance it had forged with that nation in 1778 and to back Great Britain. The Republicans favored close ties with the French, seeing France's ongoing revolution as a mirror of America's struggle for democracy. The Republicans believed that since France had aided the United States in its war with Great Britain, it was only right for the United States to return the favor.

Finally the Federalists, who controlled Congress, passed two immigration laws. The Alien Friends Act of June 1798 authorized the president to deport any resident aliens whom he deemed "dangerous to the peace and safety of the United States." The Naturalization Act, pushed through Congress a month later, stipulated that an alien must have lived in the country for at least 14 years, 5 of them in the state where naturalization was sought, to be eligible for citizenship. Both acts were aimed at curbing the French influence in America, but as it turned out, the laws scarcely affected immigration. The Alien Friends Act was never invoked, and after the Republicans gained control in 1801, it was allowed to lapse. A year later, the Naturalization Act was amended; it reduced to only five years the period of residency required for citizenship.

The only major consequence of the laws was that the Federalist party earned an anti-immigrant image, which in the long run contributed to its demise. By 1810, the Federalists had realized their folly and tried to change public perceptions, as suggested in this song:

> Come Dutch and Yankee, Irish, Scot;
> From whence we come it matters not;
> We all make now, one nation.

But it was too little too late.

The Rise of Nativism

During the first two decades of the 19th century, the flow of newcomers into the United States was slowed somewhat by the Napoleonic Wars, a series of conflicts between Europe's great powers—England, France, and Spain. Skirmishes in the Atlantic made sea travel

Armed toughs ride into Baltimore to intimidate voters into casting their ballot for the Know-Nothing candidate for mayor, Thomas Swann, in this political cartoon from the 1850s. Know-Nothings was a nick-name for the members of the anti-Catholic, anti-immigrant Native American party.

extremely hazardous, and many shipping lines suspended passenger service. In 1815, the wars ended, and western Europeans poured into the United States in record numbers. Between 1820 and 1870, 7.4 million immigrants entered the United States. Although great numbers of Chinese began arriving on the West Coast at the time of the California gold rush in the late 1840s, most of the new immigrants were from countries in northern and western Europe, such as Germany, the Netherlands, Scotland, Ireland, and Scandinavia. Those from Germany and Scandinavia were generally farming families with at least enough education to be able to read. They arrived with enough money to buy land and the seeds and tools they would need to start their own farms. Some immigrants, however—for example, most of the Irish who arrived in the 1840s and 1850s—were refugees from famines and other natural catastrophes. Desperately poor, many immediately had to look for backbreaking industrial or construction jobs in the port cities where

Catholic immigrants were the object of prejudice in the United States for centuries, and bigots created an entire body of misinformed lore devoted to the "superstitious" rites and "popish" practices of Catholicism. This piece of anti-Catholic propaganda from the 19th century purports to depict Catholic priests burning Protestant Bibles in upstate New York.

they landed. They were barely able to afford housing, let alone buy farmland.

At first, the flood of newcomers encountered little opposition. In fact, state governments actively solicited immigrants who could help cultivate the land and populate cities. For example, the railroad companies urgently needed workers to lay rail across the frontier; Irish immigrants built the Illinois Central Railroad, connecting Chicago and New Orleans, and, along with the Chinese, laid tracks for the Union Pacific Railroad. Other companies, such as the mining interests in the Rockies and Pennsylvania, were also looking for cheap labor.

But in the 1840s, that welcoming sentiment began to change, and some Americans started to object to an open-door immigration policy. Part of the objections stemmed from the anti-Catholic sentiment that many Protestant settlers had brought with them from Europe.

The Protestant Reformation was a major religious movement of the 1500s that established Protestantism throughout much of northern and western Europe— but only after almost 150 years of bloody conflicts between Catholics and Protestants. The Reformation was a rebellion against what religious reformers viewed as the corruption of the Catholic Church, whose bishops and priests, the reformers argued, used their positions for political power and monetary gain at the expense of Europe's peasantry. In addition, reformers felt that the Latin mass was no longer spiritually relevant to common people and that traditions such as kneeling during services were excessive and outdated. They believed that the Bible should be translated into the vernacular (the language native to each country) and that people should be educated so that they could read the word of God themselves. They did not accept the need for priests to act as intermediaries between the common people and God, interpreting the Bible for them and telling them what to believe.

A trainload of immigrants leaves Chicago for the coalfields of Colorado in this 1870 etching from Harper's Weekly. *Despite nativist sentiment, in the late 19th century the number of immigrants who entered the United States rose dramatically, simply because the rapidly industrializing United States needed men to work.*

They wanted to be able to follow their own consciences and to interpret the word of God for themselves. When the Roman Catholic Church failed to institute these reforms, many people in central, western, and northern Europe separated from it, forming their own religious groups. These groups became known as Protestants.

Whereas a few of the early American colonists were Catholics (like those in Lord Baltimore's colony in Maryland, for example), the majority were Protestants. Some of them brought with them their old fear of and disdain for Catholicism. But it was not until the mid-1800s that large numbers of Catholics began to arrive—Irish immigrants fleeing famine, desperate poverty, and brutal exploitation at the hands of English Protestant landlords who had discriminated against them for their Catholic beliefs.

The arrival of these immigrants precipitated a storm of anti-immigrant sentiment that became known as "nativism." The "old" Americans, who traced their ancestry to the Protestant groups from northern and western Europe in the original 13 colonies, considered themselves the country's true "natives" and therefore the only ones who had a right to live and work in America.

It was not just remnants of the old hatred of Catholicism and the Catholic Church that precipitated resentment against Irish immigrants. Many were convinced that American culture could never assimilate

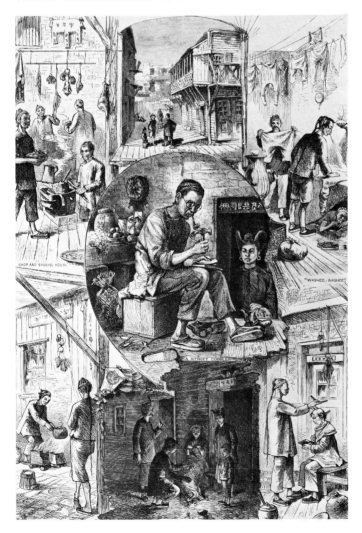

This 1877 woodcut is entitled Life Among the Chinese of Virginia City, Nevada. *In the mining areas of the West, the Chinese often took jobs that involved providing service to the prospectors who had flocked to the goldfields to make their fortune.*

the Irish because they were desperately poor and illiterate peasants with very different (and, some believed, unacceptable) cultural and social traditions. Even worse, many said, Irish immigrants had no experience with the principles and workings of democratic self-government, so how could they possibly become responsible citizens? Moreover, such nativists felt that Irish immigrants were taking job opportunities from American citizens who rightly deserved them. Eventually, this fear and hatred erupted in violent confrontation.

The strong dislike of foreigners led to the formation in 1849 of the Order of the Star Spangled Banner, which soon developed into the formidable American (or "Know-Nothing") party. The party platform of the Know-Nothings demanded that non-European, non-Protestant immigration be stopped and that all Catholics and foreign-born aliens be banned from hold-

Chinese immigrants pose on a handcar on a spur of the Northern Pacific Railroad along the Clark Fork River in the western Rocky Mountains in 1900. It was primarily immigrant labor that built America's railroads.

ing government positions. To this day, it remains one of the strangest political entities in American history. Its members carried on in a mock-conspiratorial way, like the members of a secret boys' club. If an outsider were to ask a member what the goals of the party were, his only response would be, "I know nothing" (hence the party's nickname; its official title was, at different times, the Native American or the American party). Insiders identified each other using a special signal— one eye closed and the thumb and forefinger placed over the nose. To join, a person had to be a native-born Protestant and had to swear he would always vote for the candidate chosen by the party.

In the state elections of 1854, the Know-Nothings carried Massachusetts, earned numerous votes in New York and Pennsylvania, and gained a considerable following in the South.

Some nativists specialized in political organizing.

The so-called Committee of 15 was responsible for expelling all Chinese from Tacoma, Washington, in the late 19th century. Similar committees were active up and down the West Coast.

This political cartoon from the 1880s hits at the unfairness of the Chinese Exclusion Act of 1882.

THE ONLY ONE BARRED OUT.

ENLIGHTENED AMERICAN STATESMAN.—"We must draw the line *somewhere*, you know."

Others fomented hate campaigns, singling out the Irish, who were a natural target because of their numbers, their poverty, and their Catholicism. In the eastern states, where most Irish Americans lived, it was common to see job advertisements stating, "No Irish need apply."

The hate campaigns against Catholics and other immigrant groups sometimes turned violent, resulting in full-scale riots pitting immigrants against nativists. In 1854, eight people died in Baltimore. The next year, 20 perished and hundreds were injured when Know-Nothings battled German Americans on the streets of Louisville, Kentucky. The same year, Know-Nothings killed two Irish immigrants in New York City.

The popularity of the Know-Nothing party peaked in 1856 when it mounted a bid to capture the presidency. Its standard-bearer was former chief executive Millard Fillmore. He polled 874,534 votes and won the state of Maryland—a respectable showing for a third-party candidate. Shortly afterward, a rift divided the party's proslavery southern wing and its antislavery northern wing, and within two years, the party collapsed.

The First Restrictionist Law

In the 1860s and 1870s, nativism flourished only in the Far West, where sentiment ran high against a single group: Chinese Americans. Immigrants from China had begun trickling in as early as the 1840s, driven from their homeland by a series of devastating floods and typhoons and lured to the New World by the prospect of jobs in frontier towns. Unscrupulous Chinese businessmen made a fortune recruiting (or kidnapping) penniless Chinese peasants and shipping them in filthy, overcrowded boats to America's West Coast.

The trickle of Chinese immigrants turned into a flood during the California gold rush of 1848. For the most part, the voyages of these immigrants were sponsored by local Chinese associations, which received half of the gold each Chinese immigrant mined as payment for their help and sponsorship. By 1851, there were over 25,000 Chinese in California.

When competition for gold became fierce, white prospectors began to resent the "foreigners," and local communities passed laws imposing high monthly taxes only on Chinese miners. Because of this pressure, many Chinese went into business for themselves. Some set up cooking and laundry services within the mining camps or in nearby San Francisco.

The next large wave of Chinese immigrants arrived in the 1850s, in response to the demand for labor in railroad construction. When construction of the transcontinental railroad was completed in 1869, thousands of railroad laborers were suddenly out of work and began competing for other jobs. Concerned that the Chinese were getting jobs that rightfully belonged to U.S. citizens, a group of American workers formed the Workingman's party, a political organization whose slogan was "The Chinese Must Go." Californians eventually passed state laws prohibiting Chinese from owning property or securing business licenses.

But anti-Chinese sentiment was not just a West Coast phenomenon. Neither was the rising rate of unemployment, and by 1873 America had sunk into a frightening depression. After the Civil War, Congress had begun to strengthen and centralize the role of the federal government in both economic and defense matters. In 1882, it passed the first Chinese Exclusion Act to halt almost all further immigration for a period of 10 years. Only students, merchants, and the children of Chinese Americans could apply for exemptions to this law. In 1892, the Exclusion Act was extended, and it remained in effect until 1943.

Enforcing the New Law

The federal government now had the beginnings of a national immigration policy, but it still lacked a system

Terence Powderly, who headed the U.S. Immigration Bureau from 1897 to 1908, was particularly aggressive in enforcing immigration legislation.

to enforce it. Although the U.S. Department of State had begun keeping track of newcomers in 1819, records were neither complete nor accurate. Only indirect accounting was in place, requiring the captain of every oceangoing vessel that docked at American ports to submit a report specifying the age, sex, nationality, and intended residence of his foreign passengers. A more efficient system was needed.

In 1882, the Arthur administration tried to devise one. At first, the task fell to law enforcement officials, borrowed from state governments, under the supervision of the U.S. secretary of the Treasury. The officials set up processing stations in major port cities on the West Coast, where they interrogated Chinese seeking entry into the country. All vessels arriving from Asia were required to deliver Chinese passengers to these stations. This procedure remained in force until 1891, when the federal Bureau of Immigration was created in the Department of the Treasury and its officers took over the job of inspecting immigrants.

Paper Citizens

Entering the United States was difficult for legal immigrants from China. It was harder still for illegals. Yet 10,000 or so slipped into the country between 1882 and World War I. They represented the nation's first wave of illegal aliens. Later waves arrived during subsequent years of exclusion (1918–43), but they would be lost in the flood of illegals from Latin America and Europe.

Chinese illegals got into the United States in a variety of ways. A few sailed to Mexico and then crossed the southern border on foot, horseback, or public transportation. This was extremely expensive and time-consuming. Others outwitted immigration officials with forged papers that certified them as merchants or students. Still others originally entered the country legally, as seamen on temporary passes, and then overstayed their allotted time. (This last method was useless after 1898, when the Immigration Bureau began requiring Chinese sailors to post $300 bonds in order to leave their ships.)

The vast majority of Chinese illegal aliens gained entrance to the country through the "slot" racket, which worked like this: Chinese-American citizens, whose offspring were exempt from the exclusion laws, would falsely report to the authorities that when they themselves had immigrated they had left children back in China whom they wanted to bring over. They would then sell the claims of relationship, or slots, to entrepreneurs called slot merchants, who in turn peddled them to workers in China who wished to come to the United States. Those who entered this way became known as "paper sons" and "paper daughters." A similar group of Chinese illegals, called "paper citizens," claimed and received American citizenship after San Francisco's immigration records were destroyed in the

Chinese women in detention at the Angel Island immigration station. Through most of the 19th century females, particularly single women, were viewed as less desirable immigrants than men.

1906 earthquake.

In the 1890s and early 1900s, as the anti-Chinese fury died down, some illegals left San Francisco's Chinatown and headed to eastern cities, such as New York, Philadelphia, Boston, Baltimore, and Washington, D.C. Chinese illegals had better luck there. Many opened restaurants, shops, and laundries. But like their brethren on the West Coast, they worried constantly about being apprehended by immigration authorities.

The Immigration Bureau raided Chinese communities with a vengeance between 1897 and 1908, under its chief, Terence V. Powderly, the former leader of the Knights of Labor and a founder of the national union movement. No Chinese were exempt from Powderly's raids, not even members of China's upper classes, who came to the United States for business, travel, or study. From 1904 to 1907, outraged Chinese merchants and students boycotted American goods.

Suspected Chinese illegals apprehended by the Immigration Bureau were held in detention sheds—sometimes for months—while officials debated whether to deport them. The detention center on Angel Island in San Francisco Bay became notorious for overcrowding and poor health conditions in many of its detention sheds.

Despite the prejudice and hardship many Chinese immigrants faced, their work ethic and strong family and community ties ensured the prosperity of future generations. When Congress passed immigration laws in 1965, it reopened the doors of this country for Chinese immigrants, and a whole new wave arrived. By 1980, the Chinese-American population numbered more than 800,000 (of which about a third were born in the United States). In the following decade, thousands more arrived, many seeking asylum from China's current repressive totalitarian government. By 1990, the number of Chinese in the United States had doubled to 1.6 million.

Like other immigrant groups that began arriving during the nation's open-door era, Chinese Americans today are a vital force in America's urban life.

THE DOORS OPEN WIDER

T he first great wave of immigrants came to the United States around 1820, mostly from countries in northern and western Europe. In 1880, they were joined by a new and even-larger flood of immigrants from countries in eastern and southern Europe, such as Italy, Greece, Poland, Czechoslovakia, Russia, and Hungary. There was also a rise in the number of Asian immigrants.

The most important reason for this new influx was the availability of jobs. Most of the immigrants were peasants from countries with little industrialization or advanced technology. Peasants in some countries—Italy, for example—also left because of a lack of good farmland. The United States, on the other hand, was becoming a major industrial power, with thousands of new positions opening up in factories, coal mines, and slaughterhouses. The country needed more workers, and new immigrants helped fill those jobs.

Another reason immigrants began streaming into the United States was to escape religious persecution in their homelands. Eastern European Jews, for example—especially Russians—began migrating in great numbers in 1881 after waves of bloody anti-Jewish riots. Restricted to certain small towns called *shtetls*,

Immigrants gaze at the Statue of Liberty from Ellis Island.

they had been forbidden to own land, were restricted to certain occupations, and had been denied the right to educate their children.

The new flow of immigrants also contributed to the rapid growth of U.S. cities. Unlike many earlier immigrants who became farmers, most eastern and southern Europeans—even those who had been farmers in Europe—settled in cities in the Northeast. Too poor to buy land, they were forced to get factory jobs as soon as they arrived so that they could pay the rent in city tenements. Many of these immigrants also settled in cities because relatives who had arrived before them could offer them support until they became established.

During and after World War I, thousands of eastern and southern Europeans fled to the United States to escape political persecution. Among them were Greeks, Armenians, and other Christian groups living in the Turkish Ottoman Empire. (Until their defeat in World War I, the Ottoman Turks controlled an empire that stretched halfway around the Mediterranean, from Greece to Turkey and Greater Syria to northern Africa. The Turks ruled the empire with a harsh hand.)

Developments in methods of transportation made this newest wave of immigrants even larger. Transatlantic steamships made the voyage across the ocean more quickly than sailing ships had. The steamship was also more affordable, roomier, cleaner, and safer than a sailing ship.

Between 1900 and 1912, an annual average of one million immigrants arrived in the United States, the peak of the largest inflow in American history. A total of 27 million newcomers arrived between 1880 and 1924.

New Immigrants, New Prejudices

Many Americans found these new immigrants culturally very different. Until the 1880s, when large numbers of people began immigrating from eastern and southern Europe, most European immigrants to the United States had been more similar in culture to Americans, and—except for the Irish and many Germans—most had been Protestant. Most of the earlier arrivals had at least some formal education, were literate, and had come from countries with constitutional governments. By contrast, the newer immigrants often looked very different and had radically different cultural and religious traditions; most were illiterate. Coming from countries barely out of the feudal system politically, most had little experience with the workings of democratic self-government. These differences led some Americans to believe that these people were too strange and foreign—some even thought too evil— ever to assimilate into U.S. society. Therefore, they believed, these people should be prohibited from immigrating.

All this bred a revival of nativism. New political organizations came into existence, including a powerful group called the Immigration Restriction League, which lobbied Congress for a law excluding all immigrants except those from western Europe. Despite the opposition of business leaders, who valued the immigrants as a source of cheap labor, the nativists (now called restrictionists) pushed several limited bills through Congress. The Immigration Act of 1882 (approved by Congress a few short months after the passage of the Chinese Exclusion Act) prohibited convicts and persons with contagious diseases from entering the United States. It also denied entry to the insane, the mentally handicapped, and anyone else with no family and no means of support—in other words, to those who were likely to become public charges. In 1885, Congress prohibited private businesses from importing contract laborers, and in 1903 it banned the immigration of polygamists (people married to more than one spouse at the same time) and political radicals. These laws, however, actually kept out only a few thousand immigrants each year.

This political cartoon concerning the United States's attempts to limit European immigration illustrates the low regard in which immigrants were held in some quarters. The sign that the Uncle Sam figure has erected with the aid of a sledgehammer labeled "U.S. public sentiment" likens them to "refuse."

Ellis Island

Nearly 12 million of the 16 million immigrants who entered the United States through New York between 1892 and 1954 passed through the immigrant processing point on Ellis Island, a small island southwest of Manhattan. Once a picnic ground for early Dutch settlers, Ellis Island served as the nation's main immigration station for over 60 years. At the height of its activity, Ellis Island, which came to be known as the "Isle of Tears," processed over one million immigrants each year.

Disembarking ship passengers were ushered into an enormous processing hall to be examined by immigration doctors and questioned by immigration officials. The doctors examined the voyagers one at a time, but because of the overwhelming number of people they generally did not spend more than 10 seconds on any one person. After examining an immigrant, the doctor made a single chalk mark on that person's clothing to indicate a diagnosis. Those who were chalked with a symbol, such as *E, H, Pg, X,* or an *X* with a circle around it, were pulled from the line and held for further examination. These symbols stood for abnormal conditions or potentially contagious diseases. For example, *E* stood for eye diseases, *H* for heart problems, *Pg* for pregnancy, *X* for mental retardation, and *X* with a circle around it for insanity.

These were all conditions for which a person could be denied entry into the United States. As frightening and humiliating as the ordeal may have been for most people, less than 2 percent were denied entry. Those whose conditions were contagious or required special care were often held on the island in special immigration hospitals until they were well enough to pass the entrance requirements.

As soon as the applicants passed the physical, they were interrogated by immigration officials to determine how much money they had and what prospects they had for employment and a place to live. If interrogators believed that an applicant might not be able to support himself or herself and had no relatives in the United States to help, they could turn the person back.

If an immigrant's name was misspelled on the ship's roster or if the interrogator could not pronounce it (which happened fairly often), the immigrant was legally assigned a new name—sometimes a shortened version of the original, sometimes a new name that was not even similar to the person's real name.

Because so few immigrants were actually sent back from Ellis Island, restrictionists looked for other ways to stop the flow of immigrants from eastern and southern Europe that they found so undesirable.

Knowing most of these immigrants had very little opportunity to get an education in their homelands, restrictionists pressured Congress to pass a law requiring potential citizens to take a literacy test. Although Congress passed a literacy bill in 1885, the bill was promptly vetoed by President Grover Cleveland. During the next decade, however, support mounted for the literacy requirement. An endorsement from the Dillingham Commission, a joint congressional-presidential commission established in 1907 to examine the impact of immigration in the United States, further strengthened the restrictionist cause.

But the White House would not budge. President William H. Taft vetoed a bill in 1912. So did President Woodrow Wilson in 1915. Both presidents held that stemming the tide of immigrants might cause labor shortages and slow down economic productivity. Restrictionists finally prevailed in 1917, when Congress overrode still another veto (the second by Wilson). The 1917 Immigration Act stipulated that all immigrants older than 16 had to demonstrate literacy in any one language. In addition, the bill combined the various restrictions Congress had enacted between 1882 and 1917.

The Asiatic Barred Zone

The 1917 act also capped the campaign to exclude all Asians, not just the Chinese, from entry into the United States. When Congress passed the Chinese Exclusion Act in 1882 to stop Chinese immigration, the United States was still in need of cheap labor and had turned to Japan for workers. Some Japanese men had been brought to Hawaii on labor contracts to work the sugar plantations. Some had come to California with the intention of becoming farmers or working on the railroads.

Like the Chinese before them, Japanese immigrants worked in railroad construction, lumbering, and fishing, and later moved into service trades and small business operations. Also like the Chinese, their presence soon angered many white Americans, and they became victims of prejudice and discrimination. Anti-Asian sentiment grew steadily in the United States, especially (but not exclusively) on the West Coast. By the early 1900s, the Japanese "invasion" of immigrants was considered a major problem.

In 1905, a coalition of California labor organiza-

U.S. border patrolmen pose with their weapons and vehicles in Texas in the 1920s. The U.S. Border Patrol was established in 1924 as part of the federal government's efforts to restrict immigration.

tions formed the Asiatic Exclusion League and pressed for immigration restrictions. At the same time, a series of editorials published in the *San Francisco Chronicle* argued that Japanese could not possibly "exist peaceably in the same territory as whites." The controversy boiled over in 1907, when the San Francisco School Board began segregating Japanese and white students by putting them in different schools. This enraged the nation of Japan, a formidable power in the Far East. Although President Theodore Roosevelt persuaded the board to reverse its decision, he had to promise to restrict Japanese immigration to do so.

To counter both the protests from Japan and the pressure from Californians, Roosevelt negotiated what became known as the "Gentlemen's Agreement" with

These 15 men were apprehended near Bradenton, Florida, in 1931 as they attempted to enter the United States from Cuba. As the struggle to find work intensified during the Great Depression, immigrants became the target of even greater hostility.

Japan in 1907. Under its terms, Japan agreed to stop issuing passports to Japanese and Korean laborers (Japan ruled Korea at the time), while the U.S. government agreed to cease segregation of Japanese immigrant children in San Francisco schools. Enforcement of the agreement by both nations effectively slowed Japanese immigration, although some immigrants, such as wives and other immediate relatives and members of certain professions, were still permitted entry. By 1920, over 70,000 Japanese laborers had returned home.

Those who remained in California, however, continued to face discrimination. The California legislature in 1913 passed the first in a series of alien land laws. Although the law did not mention the Japanese by name, it stipulated that aliens ineligible for citizenship could not own land and that leases were limited to three years. Other states followed suit. In 1922, the U.S. Supreme Court affirmed the ban against naturalization of Japanese immigrants.

Although some Asians had already been excluded by earlier legislation, Congress enacted an even more comprehensive restriction against Asians as part of its Immigrant Act of 1917. The law established the Asiatic Barred Zone, prohibiting entry of laborers from Asia (extending as far into southwest Asia as India) and most of the Pacific Islands. What made this legislation different from earlier restrictions was that it excluded people on the basis of race, not birthplace.

The First Comprehensive Immigration Law

The restrictionists scored bigger victories after World War I. Anti-immigration sentiment had taken hold across the country. Labor unions grew vehement, citing poor economic conditions. The return of American soldiers from the war had raised the number of unemployed workers to more than five million.

And there were two new contributing developments. One was the Russian Revolution, which resulted in the Russian Communists—the Bolsheviks—taking control of the government. Leaders in the United States, like those in other Western democracies, feared a global Bolshevik plot. In the United States, this nationwide fear ushered in the "Red Scare," during which the government raided left-wing clubs and newspapers and held political trials that sent several American Socialists to jail. A clutch of restrictionist groups arose, notably the "100 Percenters."

The second development was that, for the first time, large businesses—represented by the National Association of Manufacturers, the Ford Motor Company, and the International Harvester Company— backed immigration restrictions.

In 1921, Congress passed new immigration legislation. The Quota Act of 1921 put a ceiling on immigration, allowing each ethnic group to grow each year by 3 percent of its 1910 population. The quota favored the largest and most established groups (English, Germans, and Scandinavians) and stanched the flow of more recent immigrants from eastern and southern Europe. The act also established a yearly ceiling of 357,000 on immigration from outside the Western Hemisphere.

In 1924, Congress further tightened restrictions with the Johnson-Reed Act, also known as the National Origins Act, which cut the overall ceiling of immigrants to 165,000 and reduced each annual nationality quota to 2 percent of its U.S. population as recorded in 1890. Thus, more than 100,000 places were allotted each year to people from Great Britain, Ireland, and Germany. But Italy, which at the turn of the century was sending more immigrants to the United States than any other country, received a yearly quota of only 5,802. Countries in the Western Hemisphere were exempted from the quotas, primarily because the U.S. government wanted to preserve amicable relations with Canada and Mexico.

The Immigration Act of 1924 also became known as the Asian Exclusion Act because it specifically prohibited entry for permanent residence of all persons whose national origin fell within what was called the Asia Pacific Triangle: Japan, China, the Philippines, Laos, Siam (Thailand), Cambodia, Singapore (then a British colony), Korea, Vietnam, Indonesia, Burma (Myanmar), India, Ceylon (Sri Lanka), and Malaysia. Affected countries deeply resented the passage of this act because it implied that their people were undesirable because of their race.

The Excluded Europeans and the Immigration Bureau

The job of enforcing the 1921 and 1924 acts principally fell to the Immigration Bureau in the Department of Labor. In 1924, the bureau required that immigrants register with the government and gave them documents describing their legal status. The bureau also set up the Border Patrol, made up of about 400 recruits who operated from several bases established on the northern and southern frontiers of the country. The officers were trained in law, investigation techniques,

A trainload of Mexicans departs Los Angeles for Mexico in August 1931. During the Great Depression, the federal government and many states enacted comprehensive programs for the repatriation of Mexican immigrants. Most of the deportees had entered the United States legally; many had resided there for a substantial amount of time.

fingerprinting, jujitsu, the use of firearms, and tracking and trailing.

The Immigration Bureau was not an instant success. Its principal task was keeping out European illegals, who were streaming in at a yearly rate of about 40,000. But during the Border Patrol's first three years, it apprehended a total of only 12,000 lawbreakers. Many continued to cross the Mexican and Canadian borders with impunity. Others used forged visas or used student visas long after their studies had concluded.

Still others turned to "bootleggers," sea captains who would hire two sets of ship crews. One set would include actual sailors who worked aboard the vessel; the others were illegals who paid for the privilege of obtaining classification as seamen. As such, they were entitled to stay 60 days in the United States, long enough to elude authorities and to blend into the population. Despite the risk, hopeful immigrants paid up to $1,000 for the opportunity.

The Immigration Bureau grew more efficient. In 1929, officers nabbed 20,815 illegals—the vast majority were European—and 269 smugglers of aliens. Most were sent back to their homelands. In 1930, the bureau deported 19,000, and another 11,000 voluntarily returned home. It is difficult to determine exactly how many illegals escaped this dragnet. In 1930, however, the bureau estimated that approximately 100,000 illegal aliens were living in the United States.

Jewish refugees from Adolf Hitler's Nazi Germany disembark from the liner St. Louis in Antwerp, Belgium, in June 1939 after being denied entry to American ports. The refusal of the United States to lift its immigration quotas meant that many Jews who might otherwise have been saved perished in Europe during the Holocaust.

Immigration Slackens During the Prewar Depression

Legal immigrants had begun arriving from Mexico in the 1910s. Many of these immigrants were wealthy and well-educated landowners and their families who were fleeing Mexico's political revolution. Because of restrictions imposed by the Immigration Act of 1917, the flow eventually tapered off, producing an outcry from American agricultural interests, which desperately needed Mexican labor. In response, the U.S. secretary of labor issued a department order waiving the literacy test and head tax for all Mexican farm workers. In addition, he invoked the powers granted him by the 1917 act to "issue rules and prescribe conditions . . . to control and regulate the admission and return of otherwise inadmissible aliens applying for temporary admission." In other words, the secretary of labor made it as easy as possible for Mexican laborers to enter the United States in search of work.

Still, many Mexicans who did not make the allowed quotas, knowing they were welcome employees, simply entered the country illegally. According to INS estimates, about 4,000 Mexican illegals entered the United States annually between 1917 and 1929. Most looked for temporary jobs in the Southwest. Some laid track for the Southern Pacific and Santa Fe railroads. Some picked crops in California and Texas. Some mined copper in Colorado. Few stayed more than a year or two before returning to Mexico.

In 1929, when the Great Depression buckled the U.S. economy and hundreds of thousands of people lost their jobs, many Mexican immigrants, both legal and illegal, found themselves without work. Many state governments in the Southwest helped repatriate Mexican immigrants, and between 1930 and 1934 over 400,000 returned to Mexico. Some had been living in the United States for 30 or 40 years. When World War II broke out, the U.S. economy improved, and much of America's work force enlisted in the military or took jobs in defense plants. Farm workers were in such short supply that the U.S. government began taking active measures to bring Mexican laborers into the United States.

Because the U.S. economy had been in a shambles during the 1930s, few foreigners had wanted to come to America, and the quotas established in 1924 and 1927 for the most part went unchallenged. Unfortunately, the laws, which were created primarily to regulate the effect of immigrant labor on the American work force, had not been designed to accommodate political refugees. Concerned American legislators were unable to ease quotas in the 1930s to allow German Jews to emigrate from Nazi Germany, despite reports of widespread persecution.

LOS MOJADOS

T he number of immigrants entering the United States without documents soared after World War II, but their point of origin was no longer Europe. Jobs had opened up there as countries recovered from the war. The new illegals—and they constituted the first massive influx in our history—were Mexicans. They were often called wetbacks, or in Spanish, *mojados*, because some swam across the Rio Grande, whose twisting path forms the border between Texas and Mexico. (Actually, the majority of undocumented workers from Mexico never dipped so much as a foot in the river. Both terms—*wetback* and *mojado*—were used as racial slurs.)

This wave lasted until the mid-1950s. Oddly enough, it began with a U.S. government initiative.

The Bracero Program

The American war effort drew thousands of workers off the farm. Some enlisted in the armed forces. Others found jobs in factories, which had rapidly expanded to produce war supplies. The exodus depleted the labor supply in the Southwest, so growers asked the federal government to import temporary help from Mexico.

Mexican men say good-bye to their loved ones as the train that will take them to the United States leaves the station. The men were going to the United States to work as field hands as part of the U.S. government's Bracero Program.

69

Mexican laborers are processed at the U.S. labor center at Hidalgo, Texas, in 1959 preparatory to their obtaining employment under the Bracero Program. Initially conceived as a wartime measure to ease the labor shortage during World War II, the Bracero Program lasted until the 1960s.

President Franklin D. Roosevelt responded by forming a committee that included the heads of the departments of labor, state, justice, and agriculture.

In April 1942, they settled on a course of action, and American officials sought the approval of the Mexican government. The Mexican leaders hesitated. They needed workers too. They also worried that the laborers might be mistreated, especially in Texas, whose citizens were known for their prejudice against Hispanics.

In the end, however, Mexico relented, mainly because it saw a chance for its own farmers to learn the advanced agricultural techniques of the United States. On August 4, 1942, the two nations instituted the Mexican Farm Labor Supply Program (unofficially called the bracero program, *bracero* meaning "day laborer"). It provided for Mexican braceros to be brought to the United States as seasonal laborers. The program was meant to last only as long as World War II.

In Mexico, officials set up recruiting centers and interviewed applicants. Those who passed muster traveled by train to employment stations in the United States, where officials from the U.S. Department of Agriculture and the U.S. Employment Service assigned them to individual farmers. Employers who participated in the program—most of them located in the Southwest—were required to provide braceros with housing and meals. They also had to cover the workers' transportation costs from the employment center to the farm and back to Mexico at the end of the assignment. And they were to pay the laborers wages comparable to what American farmers earned. According to the *California Farmer* magazine, it cost a rancher an average of $50 to put a bracero to work. Some 100,000 braceros came to the United States during the war years.

When peace came in 1945, American growers wanted the program extended, pointing to a continuing labor shortage. The growers, who had considerable lobbying power in Congress, convinced lawmakers to keep the program alive until 1964, nearly 20 years after the war's end. During that period, the program brought ever greater numbers of Mexicans to states as far away as Minnesota and Wisconsin.

The Mexican government wanted the program continued because of the large amounts of money the braceros sent back to their families, thereby helping the Mexican economy. The braceros favored the program because it offered opportunities not available in their homeland.

One benefit of the bracero program was its legality; the U.S. government kept records of the immigrant workers. After the program ended, undocumented workers still poured into the United States, in large part because the huge network for chain migration that had fed migrants into the bracero program still existed. Accordingly, the termination of the bracero program probably contributed as much to the massive problem of illegal aliens as any other factor.

All told, the program lasted 22 years and brought more than four million Mexican workers to the United States. The peak year was 1956, when 500,000 contract workers entered the country to work on farms in 28 states.

From Braceros to Illegals

The bracero program seemed a godsend to poor Mexican farmers. The first temporary workers often returned to their villages with glowing reports about the money available north of the border. Although the recruiting stations overflowed with applicants, proportionately few passed the screening. In fact, over the 22-year history of the program, only 1 out of every 10 applicants received a contract, according to Miguel Calderón, an official for the Mexican Department of Foreign Affairs.

The terms of the bracero agreement stated that participants were to be recruited on Mexican soil. But sometimes U.S. officials found it easier and cheaper to sign up undocumented Mexicans already living in America, mainly at recruiting centers set up near the Mexican border. Many hopeful participants who did not pass screenings in Mexico thought their chances of getting work would improve if they first entered the United States illegally and then sought out work.

The system also broke down in another way. Because braceros were often overworked and underpaid, they sometimes "skipped"—abandoned their employers—and looked for work elsewhere. In doing so, they lost their right to be in the United States and became illegal aliens. Others simply stayed in America longer than the agreed-upon time limit.

The Lure of El Norte

When the Mexican Revolution exploded in 1910, toppling the harsh dictatorship of Porfirio Díaz, it sparked a fight for land reform and improved economic conditions. The hated hacienda system, under which Mexico's rural peasantry was virtually landless and worked under a system of debt peonage on the large haciendas that dominated the countryside, was dismantled. But the civil war, which lasted 11 years, devastated the economy. Mines and factories were shut down, farms were burned, and inflation soared. Pushed by poverty and the horror of war, many Mexicans were lured by the jobs and better economic conditions of *el norte* ("the north," meaning the United States).

The Mexican Constitution of 1917, which became the planning document for a modern nation, sought to destroy the virtual feudalism that had existed for 400 years. It contained a statute limiting the amount of land that an individual could own and legalized the federal government's expropriation and redistribution of land to the landless. Land redistribution produced a massive number of small holdings of 10 to 20 acres. These small farms are barely viable economic units,

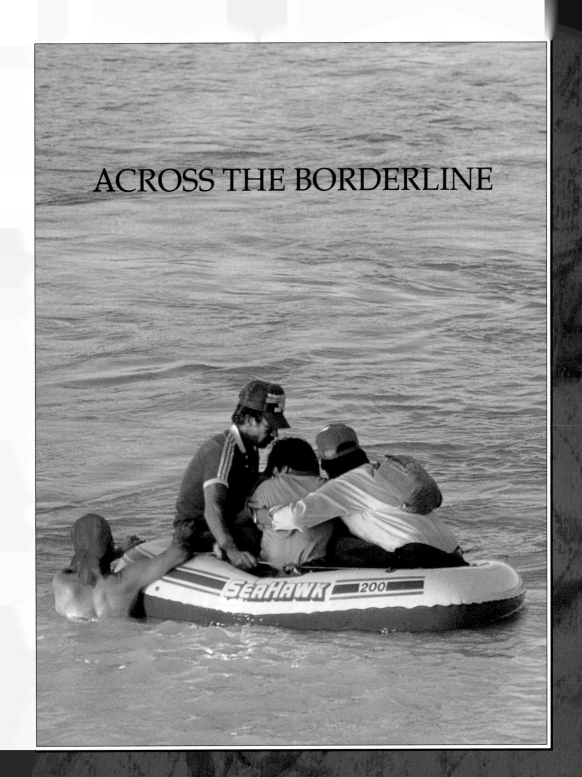

ACROSS THE BORDERLINE

In the 1980s, approximately 10 million people entered the United States illegally. Undocumented Mexican immigrants, such as these four men (overleaf), often arranged to be transported by raft across the Rio Grande from Mexico to El Paso, Texas.

Although some Mexicans enter the United States through legal border crossings (above), desperate economic conditions in their homeland spur thousands of Mexicans annually to risk the dangers of an illegal crossing. Some undertake daring physical feats, as did these men (above right) who scaled a fence on a bridge spanning the Rio Grande. Others risk losing their money and their life to ruthless guides, who often falsely promise to lead them across the border through vast stretches of arid Texas land (below right).

Even with the help of sophisticated
electronic devices (above), the INS has
difficulty patrolling the entire length of the
1,900-mile U.S.-Mexico border.
Nevertheless, U.S. border patrolmen
successfully apprehend illegal immigrants
such as these two men (above right), who
had attempted to enter the United States
through Tijuana, Mexico. Captured
illegal aliens, only some of whom are
Mexican, are held in INS detention
centers such as the one in Port Isabel,
Texas (right), while awaiting almost
certain repatriation.

The INS (below left) and immigration lawyers (above left) offer help in understanding a bureaucracy that can prove too daunting for the average person. In 1986, the Immigration Reform and Control Act offered legalization for undocumented aliens who could prove that they had lived in the United States continuously since 1982 or earlier. These amnesty provisions relieved the burden of fear and secrecy that dominated the life of many illegal aliens (above).

Restrictive U.S. immigration laws, hostility from U.S. citizens, and the possibility of a life of poverty and fear will never deter citizens of other countries from coming to America so long as it offers them greater opportunities and freedoms than they know at home. These Vietnamese women, originally political refugees, met at Camp Pendleton, California, to celebrate 10 years as U.S. residents.

and much of what is grown is used for subsistence. In addition, by law they cannot be sold, rented, or mortgaged. As a result, many farmers and farm laborers (particularly given the typically large families they must support) have gravitated toward Mexico's cities in search of greater opportunities—or looked to the United States.

Who Were the Illegal Mexicans?

No one knows exactly how many Mexicans entered the United States illegally from the mid-1940s to the mid-1950s. They made a point of evading the census takers. The only existing records were kept by the Immigration and Naturalization Service as it tried to

At the conclusion of World War II, many of the Mexicans whom the United States had recruited as workers were made to return home. These departing Mexicans had been hired as track workers by the Baltimore & Ohio railroad.

Harsh economic conditions in their homeland convinced many Mexicans to emigrate.

apprehend illegals. In 1943, it seized a total of only 8,189 Mexicans. By 1947 the figure reached 182,986; by 1950 it was 458,215; and by 1953 it was 865,318. These figures are not precise. Many illegal aliens were caught and deported, only to slip across the border and be caught again. On the other hand, the INS officials estimate that for every illegal entrant they detained, one probably got through. It seems safe to say that from 1942 to 1964 about five million Mexicans illegally crossed the border—more than the total number who received bracero contracts.

Who were these illegal Mexican immigrants? For the most part they were braceros, who tended to be single males between the ages of 17 and 22. Most grew up in rural communities of 2,500 or fewer and belonged to the class of *jornaleros* (landless farmhands). And most came from states located on Mexico's densely populated central plateau, such as Guanajuato, Michoacán, and Jalisco. Emigrants from these places reached the border by means of an extensive network of buses and trains.

These young men usually lacked formal schooling. They could not read or write, they spoke no English, and they knew nothing about American culture. But they had enough money and courage to make the long, hazardous journey to the United States. As a *New York Times* reporter wrote in 1954, "It takes more than ordinary initiative to marshal a grubstake, get to the border, and run the Border Patrol's gauntlet, all for the purpose of working harder and at lower wages than most United States citizens will accept."

Crossing the Border

The U.S.-Mexican border runs for 1,900 miles, from the Pacific beaches of San Diego, California, to the Gulf coast of Brownsville, Texas.

Those who could afford it paid $150 or more to hitch rides in the automobiles of professional smug-

In March 1954, immigration inspector Richard McCowan caught Felipe Ramirez-Perez as he attempted to sneak across the border near San Diego under the hood of an automobile.

glers. Others stowed away on boxcars, empty tank cars, and flatcars loaded with steel. The majority simply walked. If they crossed into Texas, they had to ford the Rio Grande, whose currents were treacherous in some places and in some seasons. The rough waters of the Rio Grande claimed several hundred lives each year.

Outside major cities along the border, they came up against barbed-wire fences erected by the INS. Many vaulted over the top, piled up crates and climbed over, or looked for a hole they could slip through.

Hardship and Exploitation

Once they reached the city, illegal Mexican immigrants were usually safe from capture. But then they had to find work, despite their speaking no English and knowing nothing of American customs. Most headed for the large corporate-owned ranches of Texas, Arizona, New Mexico, and California, which hired hands for longer periods than did small farms.

The first step toward such a job involved contacting a labor agent, a private operator who collected a fee from both farm owners and farm workers, often gouging both. These agents served as crew leaders for the workers they recruited, arranging for each crew to set up a temporary work camp at an employer's farm. The accommodations in the camp were usually quite grim. Those who could afford it rented small shacks or apartments on their employer's land. Those who could not were sometimes forced to construct makeshift straw and canvas tents.

The job was equally grim. Workers toiled long hours for a pittance. Growers in the Southwest often forced their employees to work from sunup to sundown, seven days a week, for an average wage of 15 cents an hour. Mexican laborers in other states fared somewhat better; they earned an average of 40 cents an hour. Some employers habitually abused their laborers by crediting them with fewer hours than they had actually worked or by withholding part of their pay until they were no longer needed to prevent them from skipping. Workers were also often badly over-charged by nearby general stores. Because they were in the country illegally, most of these undocumented workers were hesitant to report these abuses out of fear that they would be deported.

Given the low wages, difficult working conditions, and exploitation they frequently encountered, why did Mexican laborers continue to cross the border? They were not just pulled by the jobs American agricultural employers held out to them. They were also pushed from behind. They kept coming because, despite the low wages, they could still manage to send a good part of their earnings to the wives, mothers, and other family members they had left behind in Mexico—family members who often had no other source of income. The Mexican economy was largely dependent on the dollars illegals sent back to their families.

A National Issue

During the early 1950s, illegal Mexican workers became a national concern. Labor leaders blamed them for lowering wage levels, displacing American workers, and retarding efforts at unionization and col-

The lives of Mexican immigrants in the United States were often difficult. The laborers' quarters on this ranch had running water; many employers did not even provide this basic amenity. The photograph was taken in 1944.

lective bargaining. Health officials blamed Mexican illegals for increasing the rates of such diseases as tuberculosis and venereal disease. Sociologists blamed them for holding back Mexican-American citizens, who were frequently lumped together with their illegal counterparts.

Other societal ills were also blamed on illegal Mexican immigrants, including soaring welfare costs and higher crime rates. It was widely believed that they helped smuggle illegal drugs across the border. During the 1940s, the U.S. government had attempted several times to expand the Border Patrol's staff and to enlarge its budget, but all bills had been defeated by southern congressmen representing the interests of growers who used illegal Mexican labor. At harvest times, agents were instructed by INS headquarters to reduce patrols until the crops were in. On a few occasions, agents were even ordered to recruit undocumented workers. For their part, farmers, backed by a powerful lobby in Washington, pushed hard for preserving the illegal labor supply. They insisted that, without the help of Mexican workers, they would go broke.

The controversy mounted, and for the first time in American history, illegal aliens became a national issue. A flurry of stories appeared in the national press about the so-called wetback invasion and its effects.

President Harry S. Truman turned his attention to the problem in early 1951, asking his Commission on Migratory Labor to examine the issue. The commission's final report recommended that the Border Patrol be strengthened, that effective penalties be imposed on the employers of undocumented Mexican workers, and that wages and working conditions on farms be improved to attract American laborers.

Truman asked Congress to include undocumented immigration while it assembled the 1952 McCarran-Walter Act. Although the McCarran-Walter Act did stiffen penalties against those who harbored

illegals, it stipulated that employing them should not be considered "harboring." This clause was known as the Texas Proviso.

"Operation Wetback"

Yet the number of illegal aliens entering the country continued to grow. From 1952 to 1953, the number apprehended by the INS jumped from 543,000 to 865,000. In August 1953, Truman's successor, Dwight D. Eisenhower, sent his attorney general, Herbert Brownell, to southern California for a closer look. Brownell was alarmed by the vast numbers of undocumented workers and returned to Washington deter-

Even those Mexicans who entered the United States legally and obtained citizenship found it difficult to escape a life of unrelenting work and poverty. Seen here is a Mexican migrant worker and his family in their home in California's San Joaquin Valley in 1950.

mined to curb uncontrolled immigration.

In 1954, Brownell persuaded Eisenhower to launch an all-out campaign. Thus began "Operation Wetback." INS agents rounded up thousands of illegals and put them on buses to be deported to Mexico. Other undocumented workers returned to Mexico on their own.

The operation was extremely effective. In 1954, the INS captured one million illegals, a large portion of the population. The following year the figure dropped to 272,000; in 1956 it sank to 72,000. In 1957, when the number bottomed at 44,000, the annual report of the INS declared that "the so-called wetback problem no longer exists. The border has been secured." The storm had passed—or so it seemed.

In 1964, the tally of undocumented Mexicans was about 35,000. By the decade's end the number had risen dramatically—277,000 illegals arrived in 1969 alone. Ten years later, the number had reached almost a million. And 10 years after that, this second wave gave no sign of slackening.

Causes

Why did the numbers increase so dramatically? First of all, the chain migration of families started a "snowball effect"—when an illegal finds steady employment in an American city and becomes settled, he or she often sends for other family members. The older, more established illegals not only support the newcomers financially until they are able to find employment, but they ease the transition to English-speaking American culture by providing a supportive community of familiar language and customs. But new illegals are not necessarily family members. Many Mexican immigrants (both legal and illegal) provide aid for illegals through a sort of "underground railroad."

A second reason for the increase in illegals coming into the United States was that hard times had hit Mexico again. Another population explosion, this time caused by a decline in the death rate (thanks to medical advances) coupled with a high birthrate, nearly doubled the population between 1960 and 1980, from 30 million to 70 million. By the mid-1980s more than half of all Mexicans were under 15 years of age.

Mexico's economy sagged under the strain. The government made a gallant effort to industrialize the country and succeeded to some extent, but at a high cost. Farmhands flocked to the cities, which became overcrowded, and production dropped on the farms they had deserted. Although the rate of industrialization was fairly rapid, it could not keep pace with the demand for jobs. Each year about 150,000 new jobs opened up, but 400,000 people needed work. By the early 1980s, the combined rate of the unemployed and the underemployed reached an astounding 48 percent.

At the same time, American television programs, movies, books, and magazines were reaching more homes worldwide than ever before, painting a seductive picture of the United States as a land of seemingly endless prosperity and abundance.

Mexicans gazed northward. Unfortunately, the number of legal openings for immigrants had dwindled. Since the late 1950s, the bracero program had

The ramshackle dwellings of Mexican immigrants on the outskirts of Los Angeles in 1930.

been targeted by American labor groups, who objected to braceros no less than to illegals, and by journalists, church groups, and social reformers, who cited abuses suffered by Mexican workers. Growers, who now had machines that efficiently harvested tomatoes, cling peaches, lettuce, and olives, were no longer in need of Mexican laborers, legal or otherwise. Although Mexican leaders asked the U.S. government to keep the program alive, Congress abandoned it in 1964.

The next year, Congress tightened restrictions on permanent immigration. This was not meant as a direct offense to Mexico. In fact, the Immigration Act of 1965 replaced the long-standing nationality quotas with a more equitable system that allotted each country outside the Western Hemisphere the same number of slots: 20,000. But the law also imposed a new requirement, called "labor certification," on would-be immigrants from the Western Hemisphere. Hopefuls now had to prove that they had already arranged for jobs in America. Then they had to pass a literacy test and satisfy all other requirements named in measures passed since 1917. The 1965 act also established a numerical ceiling on immigrants from the Western Hemisphere—an annual maximum of 120,000.

Mexican immigrants had a tough climb. Few had contacts in the United States, and few knew English well enough to secure an American job in advance. And because of the ceiling of 120,000, even qualified applicants were not let in immediately. Mexicans did secure more positions than any other group in the Western Hemisphere—an annual average of 30,000 during the late 1960s and 40,000 during the early 1970s. Still, every year thousands of qualified applicants languished on a waiting list.

In 1976, Congress amended the laws again by lifting the labor certification, which should have increased the number of qualified immigrants. But the Western Hemisphere ceiling of 120,000 stayed in place, and worse, an annual limit of 20,000 was imposed on each sending nation. This last provision halved the number of Mexican entrants. The 1976 law abolished the first-come, first-served procedure and installed a ranking system:

> First preference: unmarried sons and daughters of U.S. citizens.
> Second: spouse and unmarried sons and daughters of aliens with permanent resident status.
> Third: professionals, scientists, and artists of exceptional ability.
> Fourth: married sons and daughters of U.S. citizens.
> Fifth: brothers and sisters of U.S. citizens.
> Sixth: skilled and unskilled workers in occupations in short supply.
> Seventh: refugees.

Those who did not fall into one of these categories rarely made it off the waiting list. By the early 1980s, the backlog of qualified Mexican immigrants exceeded 300,000. Many of them chose to immigrate illegally.

The Second Wave of Mexican Illegals

It is impossible to determine the exact number of illegals who have arrived in the United States since 1965. Estimates vary from 12 to 20 million, a range so wide as to be almost useless. The number of Mexican illegals who lived in the United States at any given time is equally difficult to gauge. The most commonly accepted range is from 3.5 to 5 million.

We can be more certain about who the illegals were, however, thanks to scholarly studies, news accounts, and government investigations. In some ways the new group resembled the first wave: most were young, single, poor, and uneducated, and they came from small rural towns in central Mexico. Most immigrated to find jobs, and most planned to return to their homeland.

But while illegal immigrants of the preceding decades had wound up on farms, the second generation usually lived and worked in cities. Urban illegals filled a wide variety of occupations during the 1970s and 1980s. In Los Angeles, for example, Mexicans became a staple in the garment industry, working at strenuous and low-paying jobs. An official from the International Ladies Garment Workers' Union, Phil Russo, claimed in 1978 that Mexican illegals "make up something like 70 percent of LA's garment industry." In San Antonio, El Paso, and other cities along the border, undocumented Mexicans provided cheap labor for electronics firms, toy manufacturers, and office supply firms. Mexican illegals also toiled as busboys and dishwashers in restaurants, as maids and bellhops in hotels, and as janitors in hospitals. A sizable contingent remained on the farm, since some growers still considered them essential. Said a California citrus grower in 1975, "It's impossible to get locals or domestics to do this work. . . . We just don't get people coming around asking for farm work anymore."

In general, life was better for the younger generation than it had been for their forebears. Most dwelled in apartments and houses rather than in squalid camps, and wages were higher—usually at least minimum wage.

The younger generation had another distinct advantage: the support of the barrios, the existing Mexican-American communities that helped ease the adjustment to the foreign, English-speaking culture of the United States. Newcomers saw Spanish street signs and newspapers and heard the language spoken in stores and shops. Community networks eased the search for jobs and housing. Community centers, churches, restaurants, and bars provided opportunities for social activities previously unavailable to immigrants.

Harder to Get In

The second wave of Mexican illegals encountered more difficulties with the INS than had the first. The department had improved its methods of finding and catching illegal aliens. Agents now used highly maneuverable helicopters with powerful searchlights instead of twin-engine crop dusters. On land they no longer drove army surplus jeeps but used souped-up four-wheel-drive maxivans that sped along the border at more than 100 miles an hour. And in 1972, the INS began planting electronic sensor devices along the American side of the border. Developed for use in the Vietnam War, these subterranean devices detected the vibrations of footsteps and relayed the information to computer consoles in Border Patrol offices. The INS had also enlarged its staff; about 300 officers patrolled the border at any one time, up from about 120 during the early 1950s.

Coyotes

As it became riskier to cross the border, Mexican illegals resorted to using *coyotes*, or professional smug-

These undocumented Mexican immigrants were apprehended in southern California in 1954 as part of the Immigration and Naturalization Service's Operation Wetback.

glers. The El Paso branch of the INS estimated in the late 1970s that close to 50 percent of Mexican illegals relied on coyotes. Their fees ranged from $20 to $2,000. (In 1990 the average was about $600.) In return, coyotes promised to deliver their clients—*pollos* (chickens) in border terminology—to agreed-upon destinations in the United States.

Coyotes had various techniques for getting their clients across the border. Some led them by foot at night, others hid them in the back of vans and drove across, and some ferried them over the Rio Grande in *lanchas* (small boats).

Coyotes often showed no sympathy for illegal aliens. They were known to lead their clients to remote areas in the mountains, collect fees, and then desert them. Another common swindle was to promise to arrange jobs for the workers, collect the fees, and then disappear. Coyotes who transported aliens by truck or van often packed them together like cattle, with lethal results.

Without an effective border-control policy, a country leaves itself wide open to organized crime rings specializing in the smuggling of aliens and the sale of counterfeit papers. During the mid-1970s, as coyotes became more of a force, the INS zeroed in on them. In 1976, agents nabbed 9,600 smugglers; three years later they caught almost twice that many. Immigration officers scored a major coup in July 1982 when they snared a smuggling boss whose organization of coyote henchmen had reputedly imported more than 24,000 illegal aliens a year.

But these accomplishments had little impact. Most of those arrested and convicted faced only minor penalties. Only two-thirds were ever jailed, and many of those who were went back into business as soon as they were released. In any case, these coyotes were mostly petty operators. As one frustrated officer put it, "We catch only the small fry. The big ones always get away."

Undocumented Mexican immigrants board a plane at Holtville, California, for the return flight to Mexico on August 11, 1951. The immigrants were apprehended as part of a crackdown on illegal aliens in California's Imperial Valley by the Immigration and Naturalization Service (INS).

In the early 1980s, the INS became aware of a new category of smugglers: domestic coyotes. Usually Mexican Americans, they worked exclusively within the United States and helped illegals get from one farm employer to another or from one American city to another.

New Ways of Getting In

As the risks of sneaking across the border multiplied, some illegals turned to other, newer means of entry. One was the Border Crossing Card, which the Immigration Service began issuing in the early 1960s. The card permitted Mexicans to visit American border areas temporarily for the purposes of business, entertainment, or shopping. There were restrictions: the bearer could not travel more than 25 miles north of the border, was required to return to Mexico within three days, and was forbidden to use the card to get a job in the United States.

Policymakers in the United States distributed the cards in order to stimulate the economies of American border towns. The idea worked. By the early 1970s,

American border towns were getting at least half of their money from Mexican tourists. What American policymakers did not foresee was that the INS would be unable to develop an effective system for enforcing the restrictions placed on card users. Thousands of illegals found they could get into the country for long stints of work.

Others pass through American ports of entry by presenting false documents. A few use facsimiles of American papers they fashion themselves. Others buy fraudulent documents on the black market. For around $500, an illegal can buy a phony version of the Resident Alien Card, usually referred to as the "green card," which certifies that an alien has permanent resident status.

Documents, real and fake, also are useful once illegals reach the United States. With them, illegals can set up bank accounts, secure housing and jobs, and avoid arrest in INS raids. They also serve as "breeder" documents, enabling illegals to obtain additional forms of identification from state and local governments. For example, an American birth certificate can be used to obtain a driver's license or Social Security card.

Marrying American citizens is another way in which many members of the second wave of Mexican illegals enter the United States. By marrying an American, a Mexican illegal can qualify for permanent resident status within a matter of months, whereas for nonpreferred Mexicans, the wait is usually several years.

Some Mexican illegals are in love with the Americans they marry. Others wed expressly for immigration purposes, paying Americans to join them in matrimony. Such "fraudulent marriages," as the INS has called them, cost between $2,000 and $5,000 and are often arranged by smugglers. Couples married in this fashion rarely live together but, in order to prevent detection by the INS, usually keep the same mailing address.

Since 1974, the INS has cracked down hard on marriage fraud. All foreign spouses of American citizens applying for permanent resident status are required, along with their husband or wife, to attend an interview at an INS office. The interviews are grueling: agents ask each spouse questions about the other that supposedly only legitimately married people would be able to answer. Immigration officers also make surprise visits to couples' homes. Such efforts produce limited results. To apprehend couples for marriage fraud, the INS in essence has to prove that they do not love each other—a difficult task. What is more, the tactic of asking probing questions about suspects' personal lives seems to violate civil liberties laws.

Apprehension Efforts

Illegal aliens who were caught in the late 1960s, 1970s, and 1980s were guilty of a crime under U.S. law that was punishable by up to six months' imprisonment, a $500 fine, or both. Defendants were supposed to appear before a judge for a deportation hearing. But such proceedings were too costly and time-consuming and required more jail space than states could provide. Thus, 90 percent of Mexican illegals were allowed what the Border Patrol called a "voluntary return." This meant that they had only to provide their name and birthplace and fill out a form saying they were voluntarily returning to Mexico. Then they were driven on a bus with other illegals to the border.

The few Mexican illegals who were prosecuted usually endured a trying ordeal. Most were forced to wait several months before receiving a deportation hearing. Meanwhile, they were held in one of the four federal detention centers for illegal immigrants located in Brooklyn, New York; El Centro, California; El Paso, Texas; and Port Isabel, Texas.

Like illegals who returned voluntarily, deported Mexicans were sent by bus to the border. But instead of being released there, they were put on Mexican buses chartered by the INS and transported into Mexico.

Repercussions

As we have seen, one result of the second influx of illegals from Mexico was to prompt the INS to enlarge its staff and upgrade its methods. But the overwhelming wave of immigrants overextended the agency, leading to corruption and inefficiency and setting off a heated national debate. It was the subject of several bills introduced in Congress. And it profoundly affected life in Mexico.

In 1978, and again in 1983, the INS apprehended more than one million illegals. But La Migra, as Mexicans called the agency, was a long way from having the problem under control. The Border Patrol had grown by almost 300 percent, yet it remained smaller than the police departments of many cities. Its reach did not extend beyond the most obvious crossing spots.

There were other difficulties. In the late 1970s and early 1980s, both the news media and the INS's own internal complaint division discovered bribery, blackmail, and other rampant corruption among its agents.

Staffing and funding for the INS administrative division had hardly grown since the 1960s. Swamped with work, the INS lost track of thousands of temporary visitors, many of whom long overstayed the expiration dates stamped on their visas. In 1980, Congresswoman Elizabeth Holtzman, head of the House Immigration Committee, called the INS "an agency out of control with nineteenth century tools. Record keeping is a disaster."

INS officers remained concentrated in southwestern border areas even as illegals fanned out across the continent. The agency, powerless to stop this dispersal, reacted with occasional shows of force. During harvest season, officers set up roadblocks along major highways, hoping to catch illegal migrant farm workers on their way to new jobs. In cities, they raided businesses suspected of employing illegals. They made headlines on January 19, 1980, when hundreds of agents descended on New York City's Port Authority Bus Terminal and caught 85 illegal domestics aboard buses bound for the New Jersey suburbs.

Although most Americans in the 1980s agreed that it was in the national interest to have a well-enforced policy regarding undocumented workers, many were concerned about the reports of INS abuses. Civil liberties groups charged that INS agents violated right-to-privacy laws when they conducted their raids. The Mexican American Legal Defense and Education Fund accused them of racism and of harassing legal aliens and Mexican-American citizens without cause.

Numerous provisions are currently being debated in Congress. Ideally, a new law would provide for tight border control without undue harassment, but there are no easy solutions to the problem of illegal aliens. As the following chapter makes clear, Mexico is only one of the many countries from which illegals now emigrate.

An INS officer stands guard over a group of undocumented immi-grants apprehended near San Diego in August 1980.

THE NEW ILLEGALS

The composition of America's illegal alien population began to change in the late 1960s and early 1970s. Before that time, over 90 percent of all illegals in the United States had been Mexican. Today, Mexicans represent less than 60 percent of the illegal population residing in the United States.

The INS is now capturing undocumented residents from more than 40 nations and uncovering a whole new breed of smuggling rings. In 1984, for example, it cracked a ring whose primary business was sneaking Indian Sikhs through Tijuana into San Diego. Another ring, called the Andes Express, specialized in transporting illegals from Ecuador to Chicago.

Most of the new illegal aliens today come from Third World nations in the Western Hemisphere, particularly Nicaragua, Guatemala, El Salvador, Haiti, Colombia, and the Dominican Republic. There are also sizable numbers from Ireland, Poland, Israel, Iran, and China.

But undocumented aliens can and do come from any part of the world. Sailors from Greece and Hong Kong jump ship in American ports, Dominicans routinely slip into New York City by plane from Puerto

The week before this photograph of a street in Pabellon, Mexico, was taken in July 1987, six of the town's residents had suffocated while attempting to illegally enter the United States in a box-car.

Rico, and students and visitors from Iran, Israel, and countries in Africa often overstay their visas.

Many of these new groups of illegals began arriving after the Immigration and Naturalization Act of 1965 further limited the immigration quotas of their countries. Before it was passed, for example, the Irish had been allotted a large number of immigrants. But after 1965, the number shrank to only 20,000 people, and by the 1980s, the Irish demand far exceeded this new quota.

A new wave of Irish immigrants started arriving in the 1980s when the Irish economy took a sharp downturn. Unlike the Irish who had come during the previous century, a great percentage of these immigrants were not allowed to enter the country legally because of the tight quotas imposed by the 1965 act. Instead, they came as tourists and then stayed to live and work in the United States after their tourist visas expired. It is estimated that by 1990 over 100,000 Irish illegals were residing in the United States. Many of the men took construction jobs, while the women found positions in child care. Even though they were less likely to be apprehended and deported than Hispanic or Asian illegals, their illegal status still made them vulnerable enough to keep most of them from applying for better-paying jobs and health care.

In an attempt to gain legalization of their status and increased quotas for future Irish immigrants, this latest wave of Irish immigrants formed the Irish Immigration Reform Movement (IIRM). Their efforts were at least partially successful. When the Immigration Control and Reform Act was passed in 1986, Ireland's quota was increased by 10,000. The IIRM continued its fight and won a bit more ground with the passing of the Immigration Act of 1990, but is not satisfied with its relatively small victories and plans to keep lobbying.

For some groups, illegal immigration increased because the 1965 law loosened restrictions instead of tightening them. This was the case with the Chinese. By upping China's quota from 2,000 to 20,000, the law opened the door to the first large-scale legal immigration from that nation since the 19th century. This had a snowball effect: each year's group of Chinese immigrants reported back to their friends and family about the advantages of life in the United States, and soon more wanted to come than the rules would allow.

It is estimated that, in the 1990s, between 50,000 and 80,000 Chinese illegals have been entering the United States each year, making the Chinese the largest group of illegals in America. In addition to Chinese students who overstay their visas, thousands of Chinese peasants are smuggled by the shipload into the United States, primarily by Chinese crime syndicates known as *triads*. The trip is not cheap: Chinese immigrants frequently pay up to $50,000 and are often further exploited after settling in the United States. Most of them are fleeing the fear and repression of living under the Chinese Communist regime, not realizing that often the life of an illegal in the United States can be equally frightening and repressive.

Experts believe that China's alarming population

growth and the continuing—if not worsening—repression of its government will cause the flow of Chinese illegals to increase in coming years as they flee to the United States, Korea, Japan, and other nations.

Many illegals have tried to secure asylum upon arrival, claiming that their rights have been violated by China's extreme birth control policies.

Only about 10 percent of Chinese illegals are apprehended and deported. Some Americans feel that current INS rules are more lenient with Chinese illegals than they are with Hispanics, and this issue is another of the many under scrutiny by the commission appointed to study America's immigration policies.

Other new illegal groups, such as Haitians and Salvadorans, came for political reasons, especially in the 1970s, when civil wars uprooted millions, not only in Latin America but also in Africa, the Middle East, and the Far East. In 1984, immigration experts calculated that the number of political refugees worldwide stood at 13 million. And the United States accepted three times as many of them as any other nation.

Two major waves of Soviet immigrants have benefited from American policy. The first arrived in the mid-1970s after U.S. diplomats negotiated a bargain with the Soviet Union that in effect traded civil rights for wheat. The Soviet Union finally agreed to allow persecuted Soviet Jews to emigrate to the United States in exchange for America's much-needed grain surpluses.

The second, larger surge of immigrants began in 1988, when the Soviet Union eased its emigration restrictions and allowed 300 to 400 families to immigrate to the United States each year. With the subsequent breakup of the Soviet Union and the deterioration of the newly independent republics' economies, the rate of immigration of former Soviet citizens into the United States increased to over 50,000 per year. These immigrants were not filling a quota; almost all who applied for asylum were granted it. In both cases, these immigrants were largely well-educated family

members who settled in urban areas of the United States.

The Evolution of a Refugee Policy

Humanitarian concerns have often played an important role in U.S. immigration policy. Quotas have been stretched or lifted to help refugee groups. In the late 1940s and early 1950s, for example, the government admitted more than 500,000 Europeans left homeless by World War II. In 1956, the small quota for Hungary was waived to let in 38,000 freedom fighters who had fled their native land after failing to topple its Communist government. And in the 1970s, the United States welcomed more than one million refugees from the Caribbean and Indochina. Most also received medical care, financial support, education, and assistance in finding jobs and housing.

A female Hispanic migrant worker gathers grapefruit in Florida. Many Mexican and other Hispanic immigrants still find work in agriculture.

A border patrolman installs a motion-sensitive sensor near a popular crossing point for illegal aliens. Such devices are then monitored from sophisticated communications centers for evidence of illegal entry.

These refugees entered the United States under various ad hoc (improvised) arrangements—acts of Congress, presidential edicts, paroles by the attorney general. But in 1980, Congress passed the Refugee Act. It welcomed anyone "unable or unwilling to return to [his or her] country because of persecution, or a well-founded fear of persecution, on account of race, religion, nationality, membership in a particular social group, or political opinion." The act standardized procedures for admitting refugees and authorized the State Department to let in up to 50,000 a year. The president could admit more in an emergency.

Wars and revolutions frequently produce large numbers of asylum seekers. For example, more than 80,000 Cuban refugees have been granted asylum in the United States since 1959, when the Communist government of Fidel Castro came to power. And in 1975, after the U.S.-backed government of South Vietnam fell and its territory was lost to the Communist nation of Vietnam, the United States agreed to admit all refugees who wished to resettle here. By 1985, more than 700,000 Vietnamese had taken advantage of the offer.

Iranians and Ethiopians are two other refugee groups who have had relatively little trouble obtaining asylum in the United States. The first wave of Iranian refugees arrived in the 1970s, fleeing persecution by Iran's ruler, Shah Mohammad Reza Pahlavi. From 1979 to 1989, thousands more sought refuge in the United States, this time fleeing the regime of the Ayatollah Ruholla Khomeini, who seized control of the country in 1979 when the Shah was in the United States for medical treatment. Khomeini died in 1989.

Ethiopians also came to the United States to escape despotic rule. Emperor Haile Selassie dominated Ethiopian politics from 1916 through 1974, when he was deposed by a Marxist regime that immediately set up a military dictatorship. Civil war broke out as the Ethiopian People's Revolutionary Party fought the military regime until it was crushed in 1978. Thousands of revolutionaries and separatists from the northern Ethiopian province of Eritrea (which has since gained independence) fled the country to escape persecution in the late 1970s and 1980s.

Although Iranian and Ethiopian refugees fled to Europe and other parts of the world, a sizable number were granted asylum in the United States. Approximately 200,000 Iranian refugees and about 70,000 Ethiopian refugees have become permanent residents of the United States.

In other cases, the decision to grant or deny a certain group of aliens refugee status is not so clear-cut. For example, what if the refugees were fleeing the government of a struggling Third World nation to which the United States provided aid and support? What if it is unclear whether the refugees applying for asylum are actually victims of political persecution or are falsely claiming persecution because they see it as the only way out of their homeland? What if they are legitimate political refugees, but there are so many of them that local communities admitting them do not have the resources to feed, clothe, educate, and house them until they can find work and be self-supporting? No single country can take in all the poverty-stricken and persecuted of the world, no matter how great that country's humanitarian concern. So where does one draw the line? Haiti and El Salvador are examples of refugee situations that could not adequately be addressed by existing U.S. immigration policies.

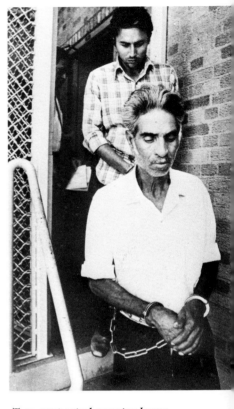

Two suspected coyotes leave a Tucson, Arizona, courthouse in July 1980. Their clients were Salvadorans who had been abandoned without water in the blazing Arizona desert, resulting in several deaths.

The Haitian Influx

For many Americans, the words "Haitian immigrant" immediately conjure up an image of desperate "boat people" risking their lives in the 1980s to get to Florida in overcrowded, rickety boats—only to be jailed by U.S. immigration officials when they arrived. Yet Haitian migration actually began in the 1950s and 1960s, when about 35,000 middle- and working-class

This drainage culvert runs under Interstate 5 near San Ysidro, California, quite close to the Mexican border. It is often used by undocumented immigrants entering the United States.

Haitians immigrated legally to the United States.

The island had long been under the tyranny of despots, but when Jean-Claude Duvalier ("Baby Doc") assumed his father's reign in the 1970s, the situation rapidly worsened. He not only banned labor unions, curtailed civil liberties, and denied freedom of the press, but he routinely crushed dissenters with his much-feared private army, the Tontons Macoute. Haiti was a desperately poor country, and when Duvalier asked for foreign aid from the United States, he got it. Unfortunately, he used the money to buy luxuries for himself and other members of the ruling elite.

Needless to say, the stream of legal migrants to the United States increased sharply, with 56,335 arriving in the 1970s and another 185,425 in the 1980s. Thousands more arrived on visitor's visas and then stayed after the visas expired. Most of the legal immigrants who arrived after 1970 came by plane and were members of Haiti's poorer classes. The majority settled in New York City's Haitian community, whose population had reached an estimated 400,000 by 1990.

During that same period after 1970, thousands more Haitians tried to migrate without U.S. authorization by sailing to Florida in small boats. About 7,800 arrived this way in the 1970s. In 1980 alone, the same year Cuba's "migration crisis" brought 125,000 Cubans to the United States by boat from the port of Mariel, another 24,500 illegal Haitians reached U.S. shores. At first, the immigrants were arrested and interned in detention camps, where they were advised that they could apply individually for legal asylum—if they could prove they would face political persecution upon returning to Haiti. Of course, for most this was difficult if not impossible to prove. As the Haitians in camps awaited the U.S. government's decision, various American civil rights groups joined together to file suit on their behalf against the U.S. government. In response, in July 1980, President Jimmy Carter created the "Cuban-Haitian Entrant," which allowed almost all the 1980 boat people from Mariel and Haiti to remain in the United States.

Carter's initiative was not politically popular, however, and when he was voted out of office later that year, Congress passed the Refugee Act to standardize the criteria and procedures for admitting up to 50,000 refugees a year.

On the positive side, this law for the first time made a firm distinction between persons viewed as political immigrants and those considered economic immigrants. Only those who could substantiate persecution on the grounds of race, religion, nationality, membership in a particular social group, or political ideology would be granted political asylum.

On the negative side, under this law, petitioners for asylum were still strongly affected by U.S. foreign policy interests. In other words, if the petitioner was fleeing a repressive regime that was on politically friendly terms with the U.S. government, he or she was likely to be denied asylum in the United States. Because the United States supported Haiti, the new policy toward Haitian immigrants allowed the U.S. Coast Guard to intercept Haitian boats and return the refugees immediately to Haiti.

In 1981, the United States reached an agreement with Haiti's President Duvalier in which he agreed to support U.S. immigration policy by permitting U.S. patrols, by prosecuting smugglers, and by promising that all Haitians intercepted and returned by the United States would not face any reprisals from the Haitian government. The agreement stood, even after Duvalier was overthrown in 1986, and during all the many coups and abortive elections occurring in Haiti before the election of the Reverend Jean-Bertrand Aristide as president in 1990.

U.S. immigration forces faced another crisis in September 1991, when President Aristide was overthrown by elements of the Haitian military who killed over 1,500 of Aristide's supporters. A massive outflow

Eighteen illegal aliens died near Sierra Blanca, Texas, in July 1987 while trapped inside this boxcar. The hole in the boxcar's floor was dug by a desperate immigrant in an attempt to get some air.

of boat people began, and by late October the U.S. Coast Guard had intercepted at least 1,800 Haitians on the high seas.

The United States faced a policy dilemma. It could not return the Haitian refugees without drawing great public criticism in the United States because the military junta that now ruled the country and its paramilitary allies were slaughtering their opponents. It was also not possible to house the intercepted migrants on the decks of the Coast Guard cutters because there were simply too many. Instead, the United States hurriedly erected a tent camp at its Guantánamo Bay, Cuba, naval base to house up to 12,000 Haitian refugees.

While they were interned, the Haitians were interviewed individually to determine whether they could legitimately claim political persecution. By February 1992, it was determined that about 33 percent qualified for temporary asylum in the United States. In spite of attempts by various American interest groups to force the government to bring all the intercepted Haitians to the United States, the Coast Guard began returning to Haiti the 67 percent who did not qualify as political immigrants. But that did not stop the flow of boat people. In May 1992 alone, another 10,000 Haitians tried to sail from Haiti to the United States.

In response, President George Bush's administration changed U.S. policy again. To deter additional refugees, the Coast Guard began returning directly to Haiti all the Haitians intercepted at sea; there were no asylum reviews, and the camp at Guantánamo Bay was closed. Human-rights activists throughout the United States were scathing in their criticism of this new policy. Nevertheless, it effectively discouraged boat people. By June 5, the influx had virtually stopped.

During his campaign for the presidency, Arkansas governor Bill Clinton called President Bush's policy cruel and inhumane and came out in support of a new policy that would review individual Haitian claims for asylum. Just before his inauguration, however, Clinton reversed his position and announced that he would maintain Bush's policy. "Leaving by boat is not the route to freedom," Clinton said. His advisors had convinced him that changing the policy would trigger another crisis of boat people and another expensive Guantánamo Bay internment situation.

The Haitian refugee situation continues to cause dilemmas even though the flood of boat people has abated. Of the 33 percent of Haitian refugees who were granted temporary asylum in 1992, most still had not been granted permanent political asylum or U.S. citizenship by early 1996. For many, the work permits granted upon arrival are expiring. They are no longer eligible for any kind of federal aid. Yet at the same time, government officials still consider Haiti too unstable and unsafe for refugees to return, even after President Aristide's reinstatement.

Since 1993, civil rights advocates have argued against U.S. policy on Haitian refugees—to no avail. The Supreme Court voted 8 to 1 that the U.S. immigration policy toward Haiti is legal and just. It remains to be seen how the situation will be evaluated in future reports by the commission appointed to make recommendations on future immigration legislation.

Alleged illegal aliens wait to be processed at the Immigration and Naturalization Service office in Atlanta, Georgia.

These illegal aliens were part of a group of 85 men who traveled nearly 2,200 miles, from El Paso, Texas, to the Bronx, New York, in the back of a tractor-trailer. They had hoped to start a new life in New York; instead, they were apprehended by the INS.

Other Aliens Struggle for Refugee Status

In the 1970s Chile, Guatemala, Nicaragua, and El Salvador all suffered tremendous political and economic upheaval, causing so many people to move to the United States that sometimes entire communities (like the population of the Salvadoran town of Entipuca, which settled in Washington, D.C.) emigrated. As with the Haitians, many more want to come than are allowed under U.S. immigration quotas. Thousands arrive illegally through Mexico each year, mostly through smuggling rings or by overstaying tourist, work, or student visas.

Once here, they apply for refugee status, generally with little success. For example, of the 34,045 Guatemalans who applied for refugee status in 1993, only 133 were granted permanent asylum. Salvadoran refugees received 63 grants out of 14,554 applications. During that same year, 57,189 people from the former Soviet Union applied for asylum in the United States, and 51,441 were accepted. Why the tremendous difference in acceptance rates? For the same reason that the Haitians faced problems: the Salvadorans, Guatemalans, and other Central and South American migrants were fleeing governments that were on friendly terms with the United States.

The Salvadorans

In the late 1970s, civil war broke out in El Salvador between the right-wing government and left-wing guerrilla forces known by the Spanish acronym FMLN. Accused of horrible atrocities, the government was ousted in 1979, but civil war continued until 1992, resulting in over 75,000 civilian deaths. In April 1990, the rebels and the government finally agreed to United Nations–sponsored peace talks and in January 1992 signed a peace treaty. Key provisions of the agreement included a U.N.-sponsored six-month cease-fire during which the FMLN was to disarm and become a legal political party. The government in turn promised to cut military forces in half by 1994 and to create a civilian police force that would include former rebels.

During this period, more than one million Salvadoran immigrants fled to the United States, many of them illegally. In spite of the civil war and solid evidence that death squads (paramilitary organizations that abducted, tortured, and murdered suspected opponents of the government) were widespread, the United States refused to grant Salvadorans political refugee status. Classified only as economic refugees, those who were apprehended by the INS were deported to their embattled homeland. This policy drew fire in the United States, and many advocate groups demonstrated—without success—for the Salvadorans to be reclassified. Other groups were just as adamant

about deporting the 200,000 Salvadoran immigrants, claiming, despite continuing U.N. reports of serious human-rights abuses, that the Salvadoran government had sufficiently stabilized for the refugees to safely return.

Finally, under a new U.S. law passed in 1992, Salvadorans were reclassified. All Salvadoran illegals who had settled in the United States before 1990 were eligible to apply for legal asylum status, providing they did so before January 31, 1996. It is estimated that as many as 190,000 illegal Salvadoran immigrants qualified.

What is particularly interesting about the Salvadoran situation is that the Salvadoran government sent representatives to Washington, D.C., and other cities with large illegal Salvadoran populations to help their former citizens file for U.S. refugee status. Why would the government go through the effort, expense,

These illegal aliens are being detained in a holding cell in Texas pending processing. Many will probably try again to enter the United States.

Border patrolman Ed Pyeatt attempts to cheer up a disconsolate young undocumented immigrant awaiting deportation at the border station at Chula Vista, California.

and even political embarrassment of substantiating the claims of atrocities? Simple. It is estimated that Salvadoran immigrants send back an average of $150 per month to family members still living in El Salvador (even though most hold low-paying jobs, working as maids, landscapers, waiters, and the like). El Salvador is an extremely poor country. The support Salvadorans receive from relatives in the United States amounts to 30 percent or more of their income. In 1995 alone, Salvadoran immigrants sent over $1 billion to relatives in El Salvador.

The Nicaraguans

Nicaraguans were another group whose immigration caused a crisis in U.S. policy during the 1980s. In the late 1970s, civil war erupted in Nicaragua between the forces of the dictator Anastasio Somoza, whose family had ruled the country since 1937, and the Sandinistas, who took their name and inspiration from Augusto Sandino, a guerrilla leader killed in 1934 by the Nicaraguan national guard. In 1979, victorious Sandinista forces established a new, left-wing government with Daniel Ortega Saavedra as president. Concerned that the new government's leftist leanings would lead to the establishment of a Communist state in the Americas, the United States set about helping to overthrow the Sandinista government.

Civil war broke out again, this time between the U.S.-backed Nicaraguan resistance, called the contras(from the Spanish word *contrarevolucionario,* meaning "counterrevolutionary"), and the Sandinista government. Thousands of Nicaraguans began entering the United States during the 1980s—legally, if they met the quota requirements; illegally if they did not—and applied for political asylum. Despite the Nicaraguans' claims that they were escaping persecution at the hands of the leftist Sandinistas, however, the United States refused them political asylum, classifying them instead as economic refugees.

About 90 percent of these Nicaraguan immigrants entered the United States near Brownsville, Texas, the American city closest to Central America. Thousands of others entered through Miami. In early 1988, they were arriving at the rate of 500 per week. Four months later, the rate had risen to 2,000 per week. Between July and December of that year, more than 10,000 Nicaraguans had filed for asylum. Most were refused. Few could find work, so the majority ended up either on welfare or living in shelters erected for the homeless.

On December 16, 1988, the U.S. government established a new policy intended to curb false claims for asylum. Those who applied for asylum in Brownsville had to remain in south Texas while awaiting the outcome of their cases, and none would receive work permits. The INS staff would be increased to handle the mountain of paperwork.

The new rules trimmed the number of applications, but they also turned the Rio Grande valley into a vast refugee camp filled with tents and makeshift dwellings with no electricity or water.

Civil rights activists denounced the policy. On January 6, 1989, a group of immigration lawyers, led by Robert Rubin of the San Francisco Lawyer's Committee, filed suit against the government, seeking to overturn the policy. In February 1989, a federal court ruled in favor of Rubin's group and temporarily halted the new policy. But in March a higher court overturned the ruling, and the refugee camps became a fixture along the Rio Grande.

A New Kind of Refugee

The refugee problem is here to stay. We have moved from an era in which the world's fundamental source of conflict is war between powerful nations to an era in which internal conflicts—frequently the result of ethnic tensions—produce a stream of refugees and threaten to embroil other nations. Bosnia, Somalia, Rwanda, Haiti, and Sri Lanka are classic examples.

What lessons have international institutions and the governments of industrialized nations learned from these crises? Are they prepared for the possibility that civil wars might erupt in any number of troubled lands? And who will accept the refugees from such conflicts?

Immigration Reform Needed

Throughout U.S. history, immigration policies have been flawed, not primarily out of racism or isolationism but because legislators have been unable to anticipate the tremendous economic and political upheavals the world has experienced, especially in the last half century, or the impact those upheavals would have on the United States. In 1990, a new immigration law designed to correct many of the flaws and imbalances of previous years was passed. Experts say it has brought about the most sweeping policy changes since 1924.

The 1990 law, however, was only the beginning of widespread changes. For the first time in history, a new American immigration policy will be forged only after intensive study and serious debate, so that the law no longer will simply scramble to correct past inequalities. Rather, if all goes as planned, it will provide the U.S. government with a fair and just immigration policy into the next century.

A SEARCH FOR NEW SOLUTIONS

According to a U.S. Census Bureau report released in March 1996, 23 million foreign-born people were living in the United States in 1994, the year in which the data was collected. This means that immigrants made up 8.7 percent of the U.S. population, raising the percentage of immigrants living in the United States to its highest level since 1940, when it reached 8.8. "During this century, the percent foreign born has ranged from a high of 15 percent in 1910 to a low of five percent in 1970," the report says. "Since 1970, however, the percent foreign born has steadily increased." Among the foreign born, 7 percent were black, 21 percent were Asian and Pacific Islander, and 46 percent were Hispanic. Mexicans made up the largest group of immigrants, with six million. Filipinos were next, with one million.

These figures do not count illegals, of course. U.S. government figures estimate that over four million illegals were residing in the United States in 1996. Most of them entered the country before 1986.

Keeping Up with the Times

From 1980 to 1990, the United States adopted three major pieces of legislation in an attempt to overhaul its

121

A federal immigration agent (left) escorts a suspected illegal alien from his workplace, a bakery in Chicago, in April 1982. The arrest was made as part of a government crackdown on undocumented immigrants in nine U.S. cities.

immigration policy: the Refugee Act of 1980, the Immigration Reform and Control Act of 1986, and the Immigration Act of 1990. These laws were aimed at rectifying the flaws and inequities of previous immigration legislation by helping to reunite immigrant families, by providing U.S. employers access to job skills not available in the American labor force, and by defining a humanitarian refugee system that supports international refugee law. They were also designed to implement a stronger enforcement system (through employer sanctions and tighter border control) to deter illegal immigration.

Despite concerted efforts to pass legislation that balances civil rights, humanitarian concerns, and the economic welfare of the nation, the laws Congress has passed since the early 1960s have proved less than perfect. One reason is that lawmakers have not been able to agree on what kind of federal immigration policy would best serve the interests of the nation. Another reason is that the laws have had significant unintended effects.

The Immigration and Naturalization Act of 1965

The Immigration and Naturalization Act of 1965 inadvertently spurred illegal immigration when it reduced the immigration allotments of certain countries. Even though the Chinese quota actually increased from 2,000 to 20,000, those who came legally to the United States each year encouraged so many others to come that the quota was soon filled. As a result, thousands who could not gain legal entry came illegally, either by overstaying temporary visas or by entering via smuggling rings.

Congress could not have foreseen the rash of civil

Border Patrol agents at the communications center at San Ysidro use sophisticated electronic equipment to monitor illegal entry to the United States.

Government sanctions on illegal aliens also affect documented immigrants. Here, 14-year-old Mario Moreno Lopez (right) is reunited with his brother Oscar in February 1984. Although both Lopezes are U.S. citizens, Mario had been deported to Mexico on suspicion of being an illegal alien.

wars that would erupt in countries throughout Central and South America, nor the rush of political refugees who would seek safe haven in the United States. Nor did legislators anticipate the tremendous burden that illegal immigrants would place on states like California, Texas, and New York, or the questions that would arise over the rights of aliens, legal and illegal, in America.

The Refugee Act of 1980

Between 1970 and 1979, approximately 7,800 Haitians fleeing political persecution attempted to settle in America without U.S. authorization by sailing to

Florida in small boats. In 1980, refugee figures sky-rocketed. In addition to another 24,500 Haitians, Cuba's "migration crisis" that year brought 125,000 Cubans to the United States. That July, President Jimmy Carter created the "Cuban-Haitian Entrant," an unpopular act that allowed almost all of the 1980 boat people from Cuba and Haiti to remain in the United States. Congress passed the Refugee Act to standardize the criteria and procedures for admitting up to 50,000 refugees per year. The act stipulated that political asylum would be granted to those who could substantiate persecution on the grounds of race, religion, nationality, membership in a particular social group, or political ideology. But the law still had major flaws. Petitioners for asylum were still blatantly affected by U.S. foreign policy interests.

The Immigration Reform and Control Act of 1986

Congress tried to correct immigration imbalances in the 1980s and 1990s by passing some of the most sweeping immigration legislation in the country's history, especially regarding refugees and illegal immigrants. In 1986, after years of heated debate, Congress passed the Immigration Reform and Control Act. This law gave legal status, or amnesty, to illegal aliens who could prove continuous residence in the United States prior to January 1, 1982, and created temporary resident status for agricultural workers.

The most controversial provisions included fines and jail terms for employers who knowingly hired illegal aliens. While this reduced incidents of abuse, it unexpectedly increased discrimination. By 1990, there were reports of employers refusing to give jobs to members of certain ethnic groups because they were fearful of mistakenly hiring illegals.

Changes in the immigration laws also affected many Soviet Jews. In 1990, those Soviet Jews who lacked relatives in the United States were ineligible for resettlement in America. Most of them migrated to Israel instead.

The Immigration Act of 1990

The Immigration Act of 1990 effected even more comprehensive policy changes. From 1992 to 1994, the total annual number of immigrants allowed entry into the United States was increased to 700,000, of whom 465,000 were to be relatives of American citizens or permanent resident aliens. In 1995, the total number allowed entry dropped to 675,000. Quotas were increased for skilled workers and for the spouses or children of aliens who had gained legal status under the 1986 law. As noted earlier, the act also increased the quotas for residents of nations whose previous quotas had been low, such as Italy and Poland.

The 1990 law immediately granted about 30,000 Irish illegal aliens permanent residency; it also granted Salvadorans and other Central American refugees an 18-month safe haven. In addition, the law established an annual lottery for permanent resident visas ("green

The family of Jose and Silvia Carmona faced an unusual problem in June 1984. Once this photograph was published in a Kansas City newspaper as part of a story detailing how the Carmonas had won a house, it was only a matter of time before immigration officials determined that the Carmonas were illegal aliens.

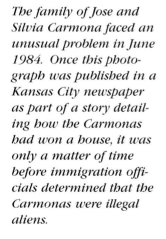

cards," a misnomer, for these cards have not been green since World War II. The most recent "green cards" are actually pink). Each year between 1991 and 1994, the lottery distributed 40,000 permanent resident visas, 40 percent of which were reserved for Irish immigrants. Some earlier restrictions, including the exclusion of people with AIDS, were relaxed.

The Green Card Lottery

Congress had established the lottery as part of the Immigration and Naturalization Act of 1990 as a way to compensate for earlier quota laws that were unfair to certain countries. Each year, between February 12 and March 12, eligible illegal immigrants can fill out applications for the lottery. Then 55,000 (the number established since 1995) of these applicants are granted a

Colonia Libertad, a suburb of Tijuana, Mexico, sprawls almost across the U.S. border, which is marked by the concrete post in the foreground at right. One of the ravines in the hills in the background is called Dead Man's Canyon; it is a haven for bandits who lie in wait for illegal aliens crossing into the United States.

Squatters' shacks in Juarez, Mexico, just across the border from El Paso, Texas. In the early 1980s, 20 percent of Juarez's population lived in homes like these; nevertheless, Juarez was seen as a haven of prosperity because of the presence of American factories there.

green card and permanent legal resident status. In 1995, over 4.5 million people applied for the 55,000 available visas.

Most of the people who filed for a green card in 1995 were not even eligible for the drawing. By law, 81 percent of the permanent resident visas have to be awarded to immigrants from countries that sent fewer that 50,000 people to the United States. within the five previous years. That meant most of the visas went to illegal immigrants from Europe and Africa, with the remaining 19 percent divided up between applicants from Asia, Latin America, and Oceania (which includes Australia and New Zealand).

Immigrants from some countries are excluded from the lottery altogether: China, Taiwan, India, the

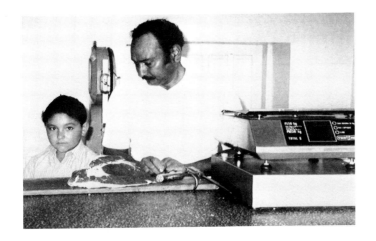

Despite all the obstacles they face, most illegal aliens endure, sustained by the hope that their perseverance will make a better life for their children. Shown here in 1987 is Manuel Sanchez and his son Americo, in the butcher shop Sanchez bought in Mexico with money he saved while working illegally in the United States.

Philippines, Vietnam, South Korea, the United Kingdom (except for Northern Ireland), Canada, Mexico, Jamaica, El Salvador, Colombia, and the Dominican Republic.

An immigrant is not eligible to apply for the lottery simply because he or she hails from an approved country. Also required is either a high school diploma or five years of experience in a field requiring at least two years of training.

For many immigrants, the lottery is the only chance to get a green card, because by law most green cards go to the immediate relatives of American citizens and to permanent legal residents, to those with specialized skills, or to people with at least $1 million to invest in American industry.

In 1995, in an effort to make green cards more difficult to counterfeit, the Immigration and Naturalization Service announced that permanent resident aliens with an old Form I-151 "Green Card," issued before 1979, must obtain a new card, Form I-551 Alien Registration Receipt Card, by March 20, 1996.

Worth the Risk

In addition to amnesty laws, lotteries, and a liberalized refugee policy, which have granted legal status to many illegals over the past 10 to 15 years, illegals have also enjoyed an array of legal rights in the United States. Before the passage of the 1986 Immigration Reform and Control Act, for example, U.S. law stipulated that illegals were entitled to all the protections of Title VII of the Civil Rights Act; in other words, they could not be discriminated against on the basis of race, national origin, sex, age, or politics. When the 1986 law ruled that employers were no longer allowed to hire illegal aliens, employers who did and were caught not only had to pay stiff penalties, they had to make restitution to any illegal employees whom they may have underpaid. Although the illegal aliens lost their jobs as a result of this law, they were entitled under American law to the difference in back pay for the entire period of discrimination, had they been paid less than minimum wage or less than a legal employee holding a similar job was paid. That meant that, even though they were illegal residents of the United States, they still had the legal right to sue their former employers for discrimination.

Illegals are also entitled under law to other important benefits. In almost all states, even if a mother is in the United States illegally, she is entitled to free prenatal care and a broad range of postnatal social services. The U.S. Supreme Court ruled in 1982 that all children of illegal aliens are entitled to a public education at least through the 12th grade, and in some cases beyond.

Many U.S. citizens who are concerned about the increasing tax burden generated by these benefits are pushing for legislation that will make illegal immigrants ineligible for health, educational, and social services. Some are going so far as to say that legal immigrants should be denied access to these services as well, even though legal residents pay the same taxes as U.S. citizens and support the economy as active consumers.

A group of Southeast Asian immigrants attend a meeting of the Commission on Human Rights in Revere, Massachusetts, in September 1985. More than 650,000 Southeast Asian refugees entered the United States between 1975 and 1985.

The Controversial Proposition 187

The expense of providing social benefits to illegals over more than a decade has been especially staggering to states such as California, Florida, Texas, and New York, which bear the brunt of illegal populations. Whether or not these benefits should continue to be made available has become a hotly debated political issue. And nowhere has the debate been more heated than in California. Eliminating illegals' eligibility for social services has become the cornerstone of California's S.O.S. (Save Our State) initiative and the cause for drafting anti-immigration legislation, such as California's controversial Proposition 187.

In this 1994 referendum, California voters overwhelmingly supported a measure that would have denied illegal immigrants a broad array of welfare benefits and state services, including nonemergency medical help and schooling. However, a federal judge blocked its implementation and later declared most of its provisions unconstitutional.

Pending Legislation

One proposed piece of immigration legistation under intense debate in Congress in 1996 was a bill, sponsored by Republican congressmen Alan Simpson of Wyoming and Lamar Smith of Texas, known as the Immigration in the National Interest Act. The most extensive immigration legislation proposed in 30 years, its provisions would crack down on illegal aliens by increasing the number of Border Patrol officers and federal prosecutors handling alien-smuggling cases. The bill also set a goal of reducing the number of legal immigrants by more than 30 percent after a period of five years, and would cap the number of political refugees allowed to enter the country at 50,000 per year.

Another controversial immigration provision being debated in 1996 was the education of the children of illegal aliens. The Supreme Court ruled in 1982 that illegal immigrants' children were entitled to a public education, and federal courts interpreted the ruling to mean that the states must accommodate the children from kindergarten through the 12th grade. But House Speaker Newt Gingrich criticized the requirement as a magnet for illegal aliens and an unfair financial burden on states. California alone, he said, was spending $1.7 billion a year to educate more than 300,000 illegal immigrant pupils.

Other controversial issues included empowering state and local police—not just INS officials—to arrest and detain suspected illegal aliens, and proposing mandatory English proficiency tests for legal immigrants. In December 1995, a House panel actually began considering a new and unusual idea to discourage illegal immigration: amending the Constitution to end the automatic grant of citizenship to everyone born in the United States. The proposal would deny citizenship to children born in the United States if their parents were illegal aliens. To accomplish that, however, Congress would have to repeal part of the

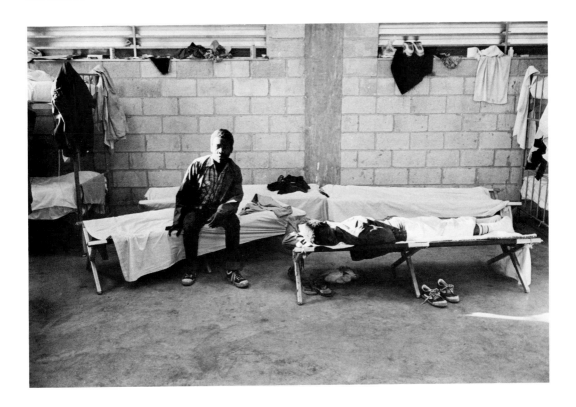

Fourteenth Amendment. Another idea proposed for curbing illegal immigration is the reinstatement of a guest-worker or bracero program such as the one the United States conducted from the mid-1940s to the mid-1960s.

Meanwhile, the Clinton administration had formulated its own immigration policy. In his Report to Congress in 1994, President Clinton announced that his administration's goal was to have Congress pass a series of laws to strengthen border control, deport criminal aliens, develop a computerized criminal-alien tracking center, make it harder for illegal aliens to find work, stop nonpolitical refugees from being granted asylum, revitalize the INS, and encourage legal aliens to become naturalized citizens. As part of a broad crackdown on illegal immigration, Clinton vowed on May 6,

Undocumented Haitian immigrants await processing at the Krone Detention Center outside Miami, Florida.

One hundred ninety-three Haitian refugees aboard their sinking 30-foot vessel await rescue by the U.S. Coast Guard in October 1980. Desperate to reach the United States, Haitian emigrants often attempted to reach the Florida coast in barely seaworthy vessels.

1995, to press for the deportation of up to 100,000 illegal immigrants in a huge backlog of cases and to step up enforcement of immigration laws at the border and in the courts.

The Immigration Commission's Recommendations

Realizing that the nation's immigration issues needed to be studied in depth by an impartial commission before the enactment of further legislation, Congress announced in 1990 the creation of a special commission to study the issue over several years and then to recommend reforms that would be in the best interests of the country as a whole. The chairman of the nine-member commission was to be appointed by the president, and two members each were to be appointed by the Speaker and the Minority Leader of the House of Representatives and the Majority and

Minority Leaders of the Senate. The commission's purpose was to analyze the failures of the nation's existing immigration policy and to make recommendations for improvement.

The commission's recommendations have not met with universal approval, however. In September 1994, the commission's chairwoman, University of Texas professor and former congresswoman Barbara Jordan, released the first of a planned series of reports to Congress. Jordan and her colleagues were careful not to claim any quick fix for the problem of illegal immigration. Instead, they recommended a carefully balanced mix of measures that would strengthen America's capacity to prevent illegals from entering the country, make it harder for them to find work, and define sensible national principles for deciding which welfare benefits and social services immigrants should receive.

The report contained seven specific recommendations regarding the curbing of illegal immigration:

Border Management. Among other suggestions, the report recommended increased resources for training border control officers, increased use of fences, improved technology (such as sensors and infrared scopes) to aid in monitoring borders, and the authorization of border guards to collect entry fees at the U.S.–Mexican border. It also recommended stepped-up security systems at airports to allow airlines to identify and refuse service to aliens seeking to enter the United States using fraudulent documents, as well as expanded prevention and apprehension strategies to deter organized smuggling operations.

Worksite Enforcement. The commission recommended using a computerized alien-registration system to reduce the potential for hiring illegals with fraudulent paperwork, while at the same time guaranteeing privacy rights and civil liberties of employees;

Double jackpot: On April 29, 1989, Justo Ricardo Somaribba, a Nicaraguan immigrant, won Florida's state lottery. Four days later, his request for political asylum was granted, meaning that he and his family would be allowed to remain in the United States.

stricter enforcement of employer sanctions and wage/hour, child labor, and other labor standards; and strategies to eliminate discrimination by employers who avoid hiring minorities out of fear of hiring illegals.

Benefits Eligibility and Fiscal Impact. The report urged Congress to refuse to provide illegal immigrants with most forms of public aid, with exceptions such as emergency medical care, immunizations, and school lunches. The report proposed strengthening requirements that families be held responsible for supporting the legal immigrants who are admitted to this country because they are spouses, children, parents, or siblings of citizens and permanent residents. But it would not prohibit them from receiving welfare. One aim of the recommendations was to reduce the number of immigrants collecting Supplemental Security Income (SSI) benefits, intended for the disabled and elderly (immigrants on SSI rolls have jumped from 100,000 to 700,000 in the last decade).

Detention and Removal of Illegal Aliens. The commission recommended increased resources for INS investigations to identify and deport criminal aliens, the drafting of bilateral treaties with Mexico and other countries to encourage the transfer of criminal aliens to serve sentences in their own countries, and the repatriation of deported Mexican criminal aliens to the area of Mexico from which they came, rather than simply to the border.

Immigration Emergencies. The commission stated that a credible immigration policy requires the ability to respond effectively and humanely to immigration emergencies, but it deferred to a later report making specific recommendations regarding contingency planning, interdiction, safe havens, asylum procedures, temporary protected status, aid to communities experiencing emergency arrivals of aliens, and other issues.

Curtailing Unlawful Immigration at the Source. The commission recommended that the United States give priority in its foreign policy and international economic policy to long-term reduction in the causes of unauthorized migration to America. This should include the creation of international and cooperative organizations to discuss immigration and its impact on international trade and political relations, the creation of domestic intelligence-gathering organizations that can anticipate the early signs of emerging

Colombian immigrant Zoraida Naranjo helps her friend, Guillermo Galliano, with the paperwork necessary to apply for citizenship under the INS amnesty program. Naranjo likened residing in the United States illegally to "being in a big prison."

illegal immigration movements, and the coordinated efforts of nations (especially those in the Western Hemisphere) to take specific steps to avert unauthorized migration.

Improving Data. The most controversial recommendation—for a pilot program to test the feasibility of a computerized national registry of workers' Social Security numbers, so employers could find out readily if they were about to hire an illegal—was immediately criticized by the Clinton administration and others.

The commission stressed that it is essential for the nation to address the problem of illegal immigration. In the words of its chairwoman, Barbara Jordan:

> It is not a cliché to say we are a nation of immigrants. . . . We hold the Statue of Liberty and the words of Emma Lazarus out there to the world.
>
> Now, when economic conditions become a little stringent, we look around for someone to blame. Right now, the immigrant is the one getting the blame for whatever the social ill is. It is immigrant-bashing and it is, in my opinion, an outrage for the kind of nation we are. . . .
>
> The legitimate problem that must be addressed is that we are not only a nation of immigrants, we also believe in the rule of law. If we believe in the rule of law, then people should not be able to get into this country if they violate the law. Illegal aliens . . . break the law to get in. And any nation worth its salt must control its borders.
>
> Now, if we are what we claim to be in our mottos, then why don't we reinforce our identity as an accepting and caring people and try to deal reasonably and rationally with the real issues. . . . I think it is time for reason and logic to prevail. What we are dealing with here is nothing less than the definition of America.

FURTHER READING

Chen, Jack. *The Chinese of America*. San Francisco: Harper & Row, 1980.

Conover, Ted. *Coyotes: A Journey Through the Secret World of America's Illegal Aliens*. New York: Vintage, 1987.

Crewdson, John. *The Tarnished Door*. New York: Times Books, 1983.

Galarza, Ernesto. *Merchants of Labor: The Mexican Bracero Story*. Santa Barbara, CA: McNally and Loftin, 1964.

García, Juan Ramón. *Operation Wetback: The Mass Deportation of Mexican Undocumented Workers in 1954*. Westport, CT: Greenwood Press, 1980.

Hall, Douglas Kent. *The Border: Life on the Line*. New York: Abbeville, 1988.

Halsell, Grace. *The Illegals*. New York: Stein & Day, 1978.

Johnson, Kenneth A. *Illegal Aliens in the Western Hemisphere*. New York: Praeger, 1981.

LeMay, Michael. *From Open Door to Dutch Door: An Analysis of U.S. Immigration Policy Since 1820*. New York: Praeger, 1987.

Lewis, Sasha G. *Slave Trade Today: American Exploitation of Illegal Aliens*. Boston: Beacon Press, 1979.

Senate Committee on the Judiciary. *A History of the Immigration and Naturalization Service*. Washington, DC: Government Printing Office, 1980.

INDEX

PICTURE CREDITS

AP/Wide World Photos: pp. 18, 22, 33, 64, 65, 70, 73, 78 (bottom), 81, 82, 87, 89, 95, 100-101, 102, 107, 113, 116, 122, 124, 126, 127, 128, 129, 134, 136, 137; Brown Brothers: p. 54; The Bettmann Archive: pp. 45, 46; The Border Patrol Museum: pp. 60, 93, 106; The Border Patrol Service Committee: p. 108; Chinese Culture Foundation Collection, Asian American Studies Library, University of California at Berkeley: p. 52; Immigration & Naturalization Service: pp. 74, 75 (bottom), 76 (top); Library of Congress: pp. 44, 48, 50; Maryland Historical Society: p. 41; National Archives: pp. 36, 68, 85; National Park Service, Statue of Liberty National Monument: p. 57; New York Historical Society: p. 39; New York Public Library Collection: p. 42; Photo by Gary Monroe: p. 133; Photo Edit: pp. 75 (top; photo by Tony O'Brien), 76-77 (bottom; photo by Paul Conklin), 78 (top; photo by Mary Kate Denny), 80 (photo by M. Richards); Picture Group: pp. 77 (top; photo by Bill Gentile), 79 (photo by Dan Ford Connolly); UPI/Bettmann Newsphotos: pp. 12-13, 28, 61, 83, 110, 112, 115, 120, 123, 131.

PIERRE HAUSER, a New York-based writer specializing in American history, has a bachelor of arts degree in history from Yale University and a master's degree in history from Columbia University, where he is a doctoral candidate in history. He has worked as a book editor in New York, a park ranger in the Southwest, and a reporter for several San Francisco-area newspapers, including the Pulitzer Prize-winning *Point Reyes Light*. He is the author of *The Community Builders: From the End of Reconstruction to the Atlanta Compromise* and *Great Ambitions: From the "Separate but Equal" Doctrine to the Birth of the NAACP* in Chelsea House's *Milestones In Black American History* series.

DANIEL PATRICK MOYNIHAN is the senior United States senator from New York. He is also the only person in American history to serve in the cabinets or subcabinets of four successive presidents—Kennedy, Johnson, Nixon, and Ford. Formerly a professor of government at Harvard University, he has written and edited many books, including *Beyond the Melting Pot, Ethnicity: Theory and Experience* (both with Nathan Glazer), *Loyalties*, and *Family and Nation*.

SANDRA STOTSKY is director of the Institute on Writing, Reading, and Civic Education at the Harvard Graduate School of Education as well as a research associate there. She is also the editor of *Research in the Teaching of English*, a journal sponsored by the National Council of Teachers of English.

Dr. Stotsky holds a bachelor of arts degree with distinction from the University of Michigan and a doctorate in education from the Harvard Graduate School of Education. She has taught on the elementary and high school levels and at Northeastern University, Curry College, and Harvard. Her work in education has ranged from serving on academic advisory boards to developing elementary and secondary curricula as a consultant to the Polish Ministry of Education. She has written numerous scholarly articles, curricular materials, encyclopedia entries, and reviews and is the author or coauthor of three books on education.

REED UEDA is associate professor of history at Tufts University. He graduated summa cum laude with a bachelor of arts degree from UCLA, received master of arts degrees from both the University of Chicago and Harvard University, and received a doctorate in history from Harvard.

Dr. Ueda was research editor of the *Harvard Encyclopedia of American Ethnic Groups* and has served on the board of editors for *American Quarterly, Harvard Educational Review, Journal of Interdisciplinary History,* and *University of Chicago School Review*. He is the author of several books on ethnic studies, including *Postwar Immigrant America: A Social History, Ethnic Groups in History Textbooks*, and *Immigration*.